STREETFOOD

MOUTH-
WATERING
RECIPES FOR
QUICK BITES &
MOBILE SNACKS
FROM AROUND
THE WORLD

RYLAND PETERS & SMALL
LONDON • NEW YORK

Senior designer Sonya Nathoo
Editor Sarah Vaughan
Picture researcher Christina Borsi
Production David Hearn
Art director Leslie Harrington
Editorial director Julia Charles
Publisher Cindy Richards

Indexer Hilary Bird

First published in 2020 by
Ryland Peters & Small
20–21 Jockey's Fields, London WC1R 4BW
and
341 E 116th St, New York NY 10029
www.rylandpeters.com

10 9 8 7 6 5 4 3 2 1

Recipe collection compiled by Sarah Vaughan.
Text copyright © Valerie Aikman-Smith,
Brontë Aurell, Miranda Ballard, Ghillie Basan,
Jordan Bourke, Maxine Clark, Ursula Ferrigno,
Ben Fordham & Felipe Fuentes Cruz, Dunja
Gulin, Carol Hilker, Vicky Jones, Jackie Kearney,
Jenny Linford, Loretta Liu, Uyen Luu, Jane
Mason, Theo A. Michaels, Hannah Miles,
Miisa Mink, Nitisha Patel, Louise Pickford,
James Porter, Annie Rigg, Laura Washburn
Hutton. All other text copyright © Ryland
Peters & Small 2020.
Design and commissioned photography
copyright © Ryland Peters & Small 2020
(see page 160 for a full list of credits).

ISBN: 978-1-78879-216-5

Printed in China

NOTES
• Both British (Metric) and American
(Imperial plus US cups) measurements are
included in these recipes for your
convenience, however, it is important to work
with one set of measurements only and not
alternate between the two within a recipe.
• Ovens should be preheated to the specified
temperatures. We recommend using an oven
thermometer. If using a fan-assisted oven,
adjust temperatures according to the
manufacturer's instructions.
• All eggs are medium (UK) or large (US),
unless specified as large, in which case US
extra-large should be used. Uncooked or
partially cooked eggs should not be served
to the elderly, young children, pregnant
women or those with compromised
immune systems.
• When a recipe calls for grated zest of
citrus fruit, buy unwaxed fruit and wash
well before using. If you can only find
treated fruit, scrub well in warm, soapy
water before using.

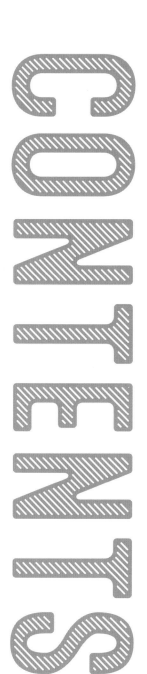

CONTENTS

INTRODUCTION

Long gone are the days of having to visit top-notch restaurants in order to try the excellent and diverse cuisine that a country and its culture has to offer. Today, with the soaring popularity of street food – ready-to-eat, portable, finger-licking dishes – you can stroll through bustling market stalls, visit street-side cafés or seek out pop-ups and foodie festivals anywhere in the world and choose from the deliciously different foods that vendors are sure to tempt you with. When you come across the wonderful aromas and first-rate flavours, not only are you guaranteed to turn your head in hungry curiosity, but you will often find that each recipe provides an insight into the food traditions of that country, and even showcase the regional variations of its most well-known dishes.

As you read each chapter of this book, you can sit back and plan a foodie adventure of your own as you discover some of the favourite and most authentic eat-me-now snacks, mid-morning treats and lunch-time bites from each part of the world. Starting off in Tastes of the Americas, you can head to the streets of Mexico for buttery corn elotes or a tasty fish taco, to Buffalo in New York for some red hot chicken wings and on to Hawaii for a modern twist on traditional seafood poke. Next, take a ravenous road trip through European Cuisine for some best-of-British fish and chips or Grecian crispy filo rolls – with a bit of Spanish paella, Italian pizza and Polish pierogi along the way! Moving on to Flavours of Africa & the Middle East you'll sample the sticky-sweet, nut-filled baklava from Turkey,

a hearty tagine from the colourful markets of Morocco and – a true classic across many regions in the Middle East – moreish falafel bites. Travel east and expand your taste buds' horizons even further with the zingy and fresh chow found in An Asian Adventure – make your own trendy veggie clamshell bao buns, a better-than-any-take-away pad Thai or a satisfyingly slurpy Japanese ramen bowl. And, finally, recreate the scrumptious dishes from what is probably the home of some of the most-loved street foods of them all in Experience India. From perfect potato samosas and crispy courgette and onion bhajis, to luscious lamb kathi rolls and Amritsari fish pakoras – they're so good you can smell the aromatic spices already!

When you're searching for a country's most-cherished and creative foods, the options from street-side vendors are varied, vibrant and inviting for everyone. So, as you delve into the flavourful recipes in this book, you and your kitchen will be transported on a tasty trip around the world to experience the exquisite yet everyday dishes that each culture does best.

TASTES OF THE AMERICAS

TRADITIONAL HAWAIIAN POKE – CUTS OF RAW FISH 'COOKED' BY ITS SEASONING
AND SERVED AS A SNACK – IS SIMILAR TO PERUVIAN CEVICHE OR ITALIAN CARPACCIO.
TODAY, YOU'LL FIND POKE IS HEAVILY INFLUENCED BY SWEET-SOUR ASIAN FLAVOURS.

POKE INARI CUPS

SUSHI RICE
250 g/1½ cups sushi rice
1 teaspoon salt
2 tablespoons white
    sugar
3 tablespoons rice
    vinegar
2 tablespoons mirin

PRAWN/SHRIMP POKE
500 g/1 lb. 2 oz. very
    fresh raw prawns/
    shrimp, peeled
freshly squeezed juice of
    1 lime
2 teaspoons yuzu
2 tablespoons coriander
    seeds
1 red onion, very thinly
    sliced
2 tablespoons shoyu

1 teaspoon chia seeds
1 teaspoon crumbed nori
    seaweed

TO SERVE
12 inari pouches (also
    called inari pockets
    or wraps)
2 tablespoons tobiko
    (fish roe)
2 tablespoons nori
    seaweed
3 tablespoons bean curd
3 spring onions/
    scallions, finely sliced
Sriracha chilli sauce
3 small chillies/chiles,
    finely diced

SERVES 4

First prepare the sushi rice. Rinse the rice at least
three times in cold water. Place in a medium-sized
pan with 500 ml/2 cups water and bring to a boil.
After the water reaches boiling point, reduce the
heat to a low simmer and cover with a lid. The rice
should absorb all the water and be tender after
20 minutes.

Meanwhile, combine the salt, sugar, rice
vinegar and mirin in a bowl.

Tip the rice out of the pan onto a baking sheet
and spread out so that it cools quickly. You can aid
the cooling process by fanning the rice. While
fanning, gently pour over the vinegar mixture and
combine by running through the rice with a fork.
Set aside until ready to serve.

To make the prawn/shrimp poke, place the
raw peeled prawns/shrimp in a bowl with the lime
juice and yuzu. Marinate for 30–60 minutes.

Toast the coriander seeds in a dry frying pan/
skillet, stirring to ensure they do not burn, then
grind using a pestle and mortar. Add to the
marinade with the red onion for a final 15 minutes
of marinating. Just before serving, add the shoyu,
chia seeds and nori seaweed.

To serve, take an inari pouch and shape
into a top-loadable cup. Put a little sushi rice in
the bottom, fill with the prawn/shrimp poke. Add
tobiko, nori and a small amount of bean curd, and
top with spring onions/scallions. Repeat to make
11 more cups. Pour a little poke marinade into each
cup to moisten.

Have Sriracha, finely diced chillies/chiles and
more marinade on the side for seasoning to taste.

MACKEREL CEVICHE WITH FRESH ROLLS

WIDELY CLAIMED TO HAVE ITS ORIGINS IN PERU, CEVICHE IS SOMETHING OF A NATIONAL DISH THAT IS ENJOYED ALONG ALL THE COASTAL REGIONS OF LATIN AMERICA AND, IN RECENT DECADES IT HAS GAINED POPULARITY THROUGHOUT THE REST OF THE WORLD. THIS RECIPE DOESN'T REQUIRE ANY COOKING AS SUCH - THE FISH IS 'COOKED' BY ITS ACIDIC MARINADE - SO IT'S IDEAL FOR ALFRESCO DINING.

FISH
1 lemongrass stalk, finely chopped
freshly squeezed juice of 1½ limes and grated zest of 1 lime
4 tablespoons orange juice
2 teaspoons sugar
½ shallot, finely chopped
½ Bird's Eye chilli/chile
2 teaspoons fish sauce
2 large mackerel fillets (about 200 g/7 oz.)

GARNISHES
beansprouts
sawtooth, finely chopped (optional) or Thai sweet basil
fresh mint
crushed roasted salted peanuts
Bird's Eye chillies/ chiles, seeded and sliced

DIPPING SAUCE
¼ pineapple, peeled
2 tablespoons fish sauce
2 Bird's Eye chillies/ chiles, seeded and sliced
2 garlic cloves
2 tablespoons cider vinegar
2 tablespoons sugar

FILLING
100 g/3½ oz. thin rice vermicelli
a pinch of salt
a dash of vinegar
4–6 rice paper/edible wafer paper sheets, about 16 cm/ 6 inches
shiso/perilla leaves (optional)
cockscomb mint (optional)
fresh mint
coriander/cilantro

MAKES 4–6

For the fish, combine all the ingredients, except the mackerel, in a bowl. With a sharp knife, cut the mackerel on the diagonal, against the grain, into thin slices. Marinate in the bowl for 10–15 minutes, turning the slices gently halfway through.

Next, prepare the garnishes. Blanch the beansprouts in a saucepan of boiling water for 1 minute.

When the fish is ready (it should be 'cooked' on the outside and raw on the inside). Sprinkle with the sawtooth, mint, peanuts and chillies/chiles.

For the dipping sauce, blitz all the ingredients together in a blender.

Finally, for the filling, put the rice vermicelli, a pinch of salt and a dash of vinegar in a bowl or pan of boiling water, cover and let cook for 5–10 minutes, until soft. Drain and rinse with hot water.

Pour some warm water into a tray deep and large enough to submerge the rice paper/edible wafer paper sheets.

Dip a rice paper/edible wafer paper sheet in the water, put on a plate, fill with the fish, beansprouts and remaining filling ingredients and serve with the dipping sauce.

PULLED PORK IS A STAPLE OF SOUTHERN COOKING AND MAKES FOR A MEAN LUNCH
WHEN SERVED WITH LASHINGS OF BBQ SAUCE IN A CRUSTY ROLL. YOU'LL NEED TO START
THE DAY BEFORE SERVING TO ENSURE AMPLE TIME FOR THE DRY RUB TO DO ITS WORK.

DRY-RUBBED PULLED PORK

1 pork rack, about 5 or 6 bones
  (about 1.5 kg/3½ lbs.)
2 tablespoons sea salt
2 tablespoons dark soft/packed
  brown sugar
2 teaspoons paprika
½ teaspoon cayenne pepper
3 tablespoons brandy
Chunky BBQ Sauce, to serve
  (see below)

CHUNKY BBQ SAUCE
50 g/3½ tablespoons butter
1 onion, chopped
2 teaspoons tomato purée/
  paste
2 tablespoons soft/packed
  brown sugar
1 teaspoon paprika
a pinch of chipotle powder
2 teaspoons Worcestershire
  sauce
1 teaspoon English/hot mustard
  powder
2 tablespoons white wine
  vinegar
a pinch each of sea salt and
  freshly ground black pepper

SERVES 4

Remove the fat along the top of the pork rack using a sharp knife, and
set it aside. Mix the salt, sugar, paprika and cayenne pepper in a bowl
and rub most of this mixture over the joint – be sure to get in-between
the trimmed bones. Place the layer of fat back on top of the rack, then
rub the remaining seasoning mixture over it. Wrap the joint in clingfilm/
plastic wrap and leave in the fridge overnight or for at least 3 hours.

Preheat the oven to 200°C (400°F) Gas 6.

Unwrap the joint and put it in an ovenproof dish. Drizzle the brandy
over the top. Roast in the preheated oven for 25–30 minutes, so the
outside begins to brown. Reduce the oven temperature down to 120°C
(250°F) Gas ½. Remove the dish from the oven and transfer the joint
onto some foil. Wrap the foil over the joint, enclosing the meat, then
return it to the dish. Pour in water around the edge so that it's about
2-cm/3/4-inch high. Return to the oven and cook for an additional 3 hours.

Meanwhile, make the Chunky BBQ Sauce. Melt the butter in a frying
pan/skillet over medium heat, add the onion and fry until soft and
browned. Add the tomato purée/paste, sugar, paprika and chipotle
powder, and stir well. Add the Worcestershire sauce, mustard powder
and vinegar, and season with salt and pepper. When it bubbles, pour
in 150 ml/2/3 cup water, increase the heat to high and bring to a boil. Let
it boil, uncovered, for 10 minutes, until the mixture reduces and thickens.
Remove from the heat and let cool, then whizz it in a food processor.

Next, remove the pork from the oven. Open the foil and test the
meat – put a fork into the side of the joint and twist; if the meat is still
solid and doesn't shred at all, it needs longer in the oven. If so, return it
to the oven and check again after 30 minutes. When it's ready, the joint
won't fall apart at the sides, but you should be able to turn the fork and
see the pork meat start to shred.

At this stage, turn the oven back up to 200°C (400°F) Gas 6. Undo
the foil and remove the layer of fat from the top of the joint, then, with
the foil still open, return it to the hot oven for 20 minutes, until the
top is crisp. Remove from the oven, slice the joint between the bones
and serve it as chops, or strip the meat off the bone, pull/shred it, then
serve in a crusty bread roll with the Chunky BBQ Sauce.

THERE IS SOMETHING SO SATISFYING ABOUT AN EGG ROLL. MAYBE IT'S THE CRUNCH; MAYBE IT'S SOMETHING ABOUT HOW PORK AND CABBAGE COME TOGETHER WHEN HUGGED IN BETWEEN EGG ROLL WRAPPERS AND DEEP FRIED. WHATEVER IT IS, THIS CHINESE-INFLUENCED COMBO – THOUGHT TO HAVE BEEN CREATED BY THE FIRST CHINESE SETTLERS IN NEW YORK – IS DELICIOUS!

EGG ROLLS

3 tablespoons olive oil
1 teaspoon sea salt
1 teaspoon ground black pepper
1 teaspoon ground ginger
1 teaspoon garlic powder
450 g/1 lb. pork shoulder
2 tablespoons plain/all-purpose flour
2 tablespoons water
120 g/2 cups cabbage, shredded
1 medium carrot, shredded
8 x 18-cm/7-inch square egg roll wrappers
1 litre/quart peanut oil, for frying
2 tablespoons sesame seeds (optional)

SWEET & SOUR SAUCE
1 tablespoon soy sauce
1 tablespoon water
3½ tablespoons sugar
3½ tablespoons white vinegar
zest of 1 orange

an instant-read thermometer

MAKES 8

Preheat the oven to 180°C (350°F) Gas 4.

Spread the olive oil, salt, ground black pepper, ginger and garlic powder on the pork shoulder.

Set the meat on a rack set into a roasting pan. Roast for 20 minutes, and then reduce the heat to 160°C (325°F) Gas 3. Continue to cook until an instant-read thermometer inserted into the shoulder reads 85°C (185°F), about 1–2 hours. Remove the pork from the oven and let stand until cool enough to handle, about 30 minutes. Shred the pork.

Combine the flour and water in a bowl until they form a paste. In a separate bowl combine the cabbage, carrots and shredded pork and mix them together.

Lay out one egg roll wrapper with a corner pointed toward you. Place about 20 g/¼ cup of the cabbage, carrot and shredded pork mixture onto the wrapper and fold the corner up over the mixture. Fold the left and right corners toward the centre and continue to roll. Brush a bit of the flour paste on the final corner to help seal.

In a large frying pan/skillet, heat the peanut oil to about 190°C (375°F). Place the egg rolls into the heated oil and fry, turning occasionally, until golden brown. Remove from the oil and drain on kitchen paper/paper towels or a wire rack. Put on a serving plate and top with sesame seeds if desired.

To make the Sweet and Sour Sauce, mix all the ingredients together in a small mixing bowl. Transfer to a small saucepan and bring to a boil, then remove from the heat. Pour the sauce into a small bowl ready to dip the egg rolls into.

RED HOT
BUFFALO WINGS

BE READY TO GET YOUR HANDS DIRTY WITH THIS TREAT! FRANK'S RED HOT BUFFALO SAUCE WAS THE 'SECRET' INGREDIENT USED TO CREATE THE ORIGINAL BUFFALO WINGS IN BUFFALO, NEW YORK. ESSENTIALLY IT'S HOT SAUCE MADE WITH CAYENNE PEPPER...PHEW!

canola or peanut oil,
   for frying
1.8 kg/4 lbs. chicken
   wings, halved at the
   joints, tips removed
170 g/1 stick plus 4
   tablespoons butter
250 ml/1 cup hot sauce,
   such as Frank's Red
   Hot Original Cayenne
   Pepper Sauce®

celery and carrot sticks,
   to serve

BLUE CHEESE DIP
150 g/1 cup crumbled
   blue cheese
150 g/¾ cup
   mayonnaise
120 ml/½ cup sour/
   soured cream

SERVES 4–6

First make the Blue Cheese Dip. Place all the ingredients in a medium bowl and beat until combined. Refrigerate before serving.

Next, prepare the wings. Preheat the oven to 100°C (200°F) Gas ¼. Preheat the oil in a deep fryer set to 180°C (350°F).

Dry the wings thoroughly with kitchen paper/paper towels. Working in batches, fry the wings for about 12 minutes until golden brown and the juices run clear when the thickest part is pierced to the bone. Transfer the cooked wings to a wire rack set over a baking sheet, and place in the oven to keep warm until all wings are fried.

Heat the butter in a 30-cm/12-inch deep frying pan/skillet over a medium heat. Stir in the hot sauce until smooth, then add the wings, and toss until completely coated. Serve the wings in a large bowl with Blue Cheese Dip and celery and carrot sticks on the side.

PREPARED IN A RENOWNED COOKING STYLE NATIVE TO JAMACIA, THESE CARAMELIZED JERK CHICKEN WINGS ARE SPICY, JUICY AND VERY, VERY MOREISH, AND THE CAJUN REMOULADE DIPPING SAUCE MAKES THE PERFECT ACCOMPANIMENT.

JERK CHICKEN

½ onion, chopped

35 g/½ cup spring onions/scallions, sliced

7 garlic cloves, finely chopped

4 habanero peppers, seeded and chopped

3 tablespoons chopped fresh thyme leaves

2 teaspoons dried thyme

2 tablespoons kosher/flaked salt

1 tablespoon freshly ground black pepper

1 tablespoon ground allspice

1 teaspoon ground cinnamon

2 teaspoons ground cumin

1 teaspoon chilli/chili powder

1 teaspoon freshly grated nutmeg

4 tablespoons vegetable oil

5 tablespoons soy sauce

3 tablespoons brown sugar

120 ml/½ cup freshly squeezed lime juice

1.8 kg/4 lbs. chicken wings, halved at the joints, tips removed

CAJUN REMOULADE DIPPING SAUCE

500 g/2 cups mayonnaise

2 tablespoons tomato ketchup (or see page 22 for Homemade Tomato Ketchup)

2 tablespoons English mustard

1 tablespoon chopped fresh flat-leaf parsley

1 tablespoon cayenne pepper

1 tablespoon freshly squeezed lemon juice

2 teaspoons prepared horseradish

3 garlic cloves, finely chopped

1 teaspoon Worcestershire sauce

1 teaspoon celery salt

1 teaspoon paprika

SERVES 4–6

For the Cajun Remoulade Dipping Sauce, combine all ingredients in a blender or food processor. Let cool.

For the jerk chicken, put all ingredients, apart from the chicken, in a blender and blend until the marinade is completely smooth.

Place the chicken in a large bowl, pour the marinade over and toss to coat completely. Cover the bowl with clingfilm/plastic wrap and marinate in the fridge overnight or for at least 8 hours.

Preheat the oven to 230°C (450°F) Gas 8. Line 2–3 baking sheets with foil and grease with cooking spray or vegetable oil.

Place the chicken on the baking sheets and reserve the marinade left in the bowl. Bake in the preheated oven for 25 minutes.

Brush half the reserved marinade over the chicken. Turn the wings over. Bake for an additional 15 minutes.

Turn the chicken again and brush on the remaining marinade. Bake for an additional 10–15 minutes until the chicken is tender and caramelized and the juices run clear when the thickest part is pierced to the bone. Rest the wings on the baking sheets for 5 minutes before transferring to a serving platter with the dipping sauce.

A CLASSIC BURGER IS SURELY THE KING OF AMERICAN FAST FOOD. HERE MADE WITH GOOD-QUALITY BEEF, IT PROVES THAT LESS IS MORE, LETTING THE MEATY TASTE SPEAK FOR ITSELF. IF YOU WANT SOMETHING EXTRA, PLACE A FRIED EGG IN THE BUN FOR A RICH EGG-YOLK-MIXED-WITH-TOMATO-KETCHUP SAUCE.

BEEF BURGERS

HOMEMADE TOMATO KETCHUP
2 tablespoons olive oil
1 onion, finely chopped
2 garlic cloves, crushed
450 ml/2 scant cups tomato passata/ Italian sieved tomatoes
150 ml/²/₃ cup red wine vinegar
150 g/³/₄ cup soft brown sugar
2 tablespoons black treacle/dark molasses
2 tablespoons tomato purée/paste
1 teaspoon Dijon mustard
2 bay leaves
1 teaspoon sea salt
½ teaspoon freshly ground black pepper

500 g/1 lb. 2 oz. minced/ground beef
a good pinch of salt
1 onion, finely chopped
100 g/3½ oz. pickled beetroot/beet, finely chopped

40 g/1½ oz. pickled cucumber or gherkins, finely chopped
2 tablespoons capers, roughly chopped
1 medium cooked white potato (about. 80 g/3 oz.), peeled and roughly mashed
4 egg yolks
1 teaspoon Dijon mustard
salt and freshly ground black pepper
olive oil or rapeseed oil and butter, for frying

TO SERVE
4 eggs
seeded burger buns or buns of your choice, toasted
Homemade Tomato Ketchup (see left) or condiments of your choice

Serves 4

First, make the Homemade Tomato Ketchup. Heat the oil in a saucepan, add the onion and garlic and fry gently for 10 minutes until softened. Add all the remaining ingredients, bring to a boil, reduce the heat and simmer gently for 30 minutes until thickened and reduced by about one third. Pass the sauce through a sieve/strainer, let cool and pour into a clean bottle and store in the fridge for up to five days. If using sterilized bottles, pour the hot sauce directly into the bottle and when cold, seal and store in the fridge. It will keep for a few weeks.

Put the minced/ground beef and salt in a stand mixer with the paddle attachment. Mix for around 1 minute on medium speed. Alternatively, you can mix for a little longer in a large bowl with a wooden spoon. Add the onion, beetroot/beet, pickled cucumber or gherkins, capers, cooked potato, egg yolks and mustard. Season with salt and black pepper. Mix again until all the ingredients are evenly incorporated (but not too long or the burger will become tough).

Shape the mixture into 4 burgers and leave them to rest for 30 minutes in the fridge before frying.

Preheat the oven to 120°C (250°F) Gas ½.

Heat the oil and butter in a frying pan/skillet. Fry the burgers (in batches if needed, depending on the size of your pan) over a high heat for about 3–4 minutes on each side, depending on how you like your beef to be cooked.

Once cooked, pop the beef patties in the oven to keep warm and fry the eggs sunny-side up in the same frying pan/skillet. Serve each beef patty on a lightly toasted burger bun with the fried egg on top. Serve with condiments on the side.

ELOTES

ELOTE IS THE NAME GIVEN TO CORN THAT IS GRILLED UNTIL LIGHTLY CHARRED AND TENDER, AND SERVED BY VENDORS ON THE STREETS OF MEXICO. THE COTIJA HERE IS A HARD, CRUMBLY MEXICAN CHEESE, BUT PARMESAN OR RICOTTA WORK TOO.

vegetable oil, for
  brushing
1 teaspoon chilli/chili
  powder
½ teaspoon cayenne
  pepper
8 corn on the cob/ears
  of corn

50 g/¼ cup mayonnaise
  or unsalted butter
40 g/½ cup crumbled
  Cotija, Parmesan or
  ricotta salata cheese
1 lime, cut into
  8 wedges

SERVES 8

Build a medium-hot fire in a charcoal grill or preheat a grill/broiler to medium–high and brush the grill rack with oil. Combine the chilli/chili powder and cayenne pepper in a small bowl.

Grill/broil the corn for about 10 minutes, turning occasionally with tongs, until cooked through and lightly charred. Remove from the grill and brush each ear with 1½ teaspoons of mayonnaise or butter. Sprinkle each with a tablespoon of cheese and a pinch of the chilli-cayenne mixture. Squeeze a lime wedge over each corn on the cob/ear of corn and serve.

Alternatively, remove the corn kernels from the cob, after taking them off the grill, and combine the corn with the mayonnaise or butter and the cheese. Top with the chilli-cayenne mixture and a dash of lime juice.

THE WORD 'QUESADILLA' COMES FROM 'QUESO' (CHEESE) AND 'TORTILLA', AS THESE ARE THE BASIC INGREDIENTS AT THE HEART OF THIS PORTABLE MEXICAN DISH. JUST LIKE BURRITOS AND TACOS, QUESADILLAS CAN BE THE BASE FOR AN INFINITE NUMBER OF FILLINGS YOU CAN EXPERIMENT WITH!

CHICKEN QUESADILLAS

CHIPOTLE MARINADE
1 tablespoon chipotle chilli paste
1 teaspoon ground cinnamon
1 teaspoon ground cumin
3 garlic cloves
1 tablespoon dried oregano
1 tablespoon paprika
½ teaspoon sea salt
125 ml/½ cup vegetable oil

GUACAMOLE
2–3 avocados
1 medium bunch of coriander/cilantro
1 tomato
a pinch of sea salt
a pinch of ground white pepper

Chipotle Marinade (see above)
400 g/14 oz. chicken breast fillets
4 x 26-cm/10-inch flour tortillas
200 g/2 cups grated/shredded
   Monterey Jack or cheddar cheese

TO SERVE
Fresh Tomato Salsa (see page 32)
Guacamole (see above)
sour/soured cream

SERVES 4

First make the Chipotle Marinade. Put all the ingredients and 125 ml/½ cup water in a food processor and whizz until smooth.

If the chicken fillets are very thick, flatten them slightly with a rolling pin. Put in a bowl, add the marinade and mix well. Cover, refrigerate and marinate for 2–4 hours.

Meanwhile, make the Fresh Tomato Salsa and set aside.

Then, make the Guacamole. Pit and peel the avocados. Scoop the flesh out into a bowl. Finely chop the coriander/cilantro and add to the bowl with the salt and pepper. Roughly mash with a fork. Finely chop the tomato and stir into the guacamole. Set aside.

Preheat the grill/broiler to high. Grill/broil the chicken for 10 minutes, turning halfway through, until cooked through.

Lay the tortillas in front of you on a clean work surface. Divide the cheese and chicken between the tortillas, arranging them in a wide strip down the middle. Fold a third of the tortilla over the filling, then fold the opposite third over that.

Place a dry frying pan/skillet over high heat. Put one quesadilla at a time in the hot pan, let brown for 1 minute, then flip it over to toast the other side. Cut each quesadilla diagonally into 4 and serve with guacamole, sour/soured cream and fresh tomato salsa.

MEXICAN TAMALES ARE LITTLE BUNDLES OF STUFFED CORN DOUGH
OFTEN SERVED AT CHRISTMAS AND NEW YEAR. DEPENDING ON THE
REGION, THE PARCEL IS WRAPPED IN A CORN HUSK OR BANANA LEAF.

PORK TAMALES

500 g/1 lb. 2 oz. boneless pork
 leg or shoulder, cut into large
 chunks
2 bay leaves
sea salt

GUAJILLO SAUCE
1/4 onion, chopped
2 garlic cloves, peeled
300 g/10 oz. tomatoes
3 Guajillo chillies/chiles, seeded
 and stems removed
1 tablespoon sea salt
1 1/2 tablespoons paprika
1 teaspoon ground cumin
1/2 tablespoon dried oregano
a pinch of ground white pepper
2 tablespoons masa harina
125 ml/1/2 cup warm water
2 tablespoons vegetable oil

MASA
300 g/3 cups masa harina
1 teaspoon salt
1 tablespoon baking powder

TO ASSEMBLE
10 corn husks, soaked in 1 litre/
 4 cups warm water for
 10 minutes, then drained
300 g/3 cups grated/shredded
 Monterey Jack or cheddar
 cheese

a steamer

Makes 10

Put the pork, bay leaves, 1 teaspoon salt and 1.5 litres/6 cups water in a large saucepan, bring to a boil and simmer over low heat for 1 1/2 hours. Drain (reserving the cooking liquid for later), transfer to a bowl and let cool.

For the Guajillo Sauce, put the onion, garlic, tomatoes, chillies/chiles and 750 ml/3 cups water in a pan, bring to a boil and simmer over low heat for 5 minutes. Transfer to a food processor with the salt, paprika, cumin, oregano and a pinch of pepper and whizz for 2 minutes. Mix the masa harina into the warm water until combined. Heat the oil in a frying pan/skillet, pour in the sauce, bring to a boil and cook for 5 minutes. Turn the heat down to low, add the masa-water mixture, stir and cook for 5 minutes.

For the Masa, put the masa harina and 1 teaspoon salt in a bowl and mix. Add 500 ml/2 cups of the reserved cooking liquid and knead for 5 minutes. Add the baking powder and knead for 1 minute. Divide into 10 equal portions.

To assemble, shred the cooled pork in its bowl, add 1 1/2 cups of the sauce and mix.

Lay out a soaked corn husk and flatten, if necessary. Put a portion of masa on the husk and flatten with your hand until 1/2 cm/1/4 inch thick and an oval shape. Put a line of the pork mixture (about 50 g/1 3/4 oz.) along the middle of the masa. Take one side of the husk and roll over the masa, tucking it in on the other side. You should now have a cylinder. Take the excess husk at one end, fold it under the tamale and tuck in. Leave the other end open. Repeat to make 9 more tamales.

Put the tamales in a steamer, sealed ends down. They should not be too closely packed. Cover tightly with foil, cover with a lid and steam for 1 1/2 hours over medium heat. Check every 30 minutes and add water if needed.

Remove from the heat, open each parcel but leave in the husk. Cover with the remaining sauce, scatter the cheese over the top and grill/broil until the cheese has melted.

FISH TACOS ARE ASSOCIATED WITH BAJA CALIFORNIA, THE MEXICAN PENINSULA WITH A STUNNING COASTLINE THAT STRETCHES FOR MILES. FISHING IS THE MAIN SOURCE OF LIVELIHOOD AND YOU CAN WATCH FRESH SEAFOOD BEING BROUGHT IN ALL DAY. FOR THIS RECIPE WE RECOMMEND TILAPIA: IT IS SUSTAINABLE AND ITS FIRM, WHITE FLESH SUITS BEING BATTERED AND FRIED.

FISH TACOS

FRESH TOMATO SALSA
4 tomatoes
¼ onion
1 medium bunch of
    coriander/cilantro
¼ teaspoon sea salt

**CHIPOTLE GARLIC
    MAYONNAISE**
2 garlic cloves, peeled
250 ml/1 cup
    mayonnaise
3–6 tablespoons
    chipotle chilli paste

FISH
125 g/1 cup plain/
    all-purpose flour
2 teaspoons paprika
2 teaspoons dried
    oregano
1 teaspoon dried
    marjoram

2 teaspoons ground
    cumin
½ teaspoon sea salt
½ teaspoon ground
    white pepper
4 tilapia fish fillets (or
    other white fish
    fillets, such as cod)
vegetable oil, for
    frying
8 x 15-cm/6-inch corn
    or flour tortillas

TO SERVE
a handful of shredded
    Romaine lettuce
Fresh Tomato Salsa
    (see above)
1 lemon, cut into
    wedges

SERVES 4

First, make the salsa. Finely chop the tomatoes, onion and coriander/cilantro and put in a bowl. Add the salt and mix well. Set aside.

Put all the ingredients for the mayonnaise in a food processor and whizz for 3 minutes. Set aside.

For the fish, put the flour, paprika, oregano, marjoram, cumin, salt, pepper and 250 ml/1 cup water in a large bowl and beat together until very smooth and slightly thicker than double/heavy cream.

Cut each tilapia fillet into 2 pieces. Gently lower each portion of fish into the batter and make sure it is well coated. Set aside on a plate.

Pour some vegetable oil into a large, deep frying pan/skillet until it comes 2 cm/¾ inch up the side of the pan. Set over medium heat and leave until the oil is very hot but not smoking.

Using a slotted spoon, lower the portions of fish gently into the oil. Cook for 1–2 minutes on each side, depending on the thickness. Work in batches – the fish should have plenty of room in the oil to fry evenly.

Using the tongs or a slotted spoon, remove the fish from the pan and let drain on kitchen paper/paper towels. Repeat the process until all the portions have been fried.

Place a dry frying pan/skillet over high heat. Warm each tortilla for about 20–30 seconds on each side. To serve, layer up the ingredients over the tortillas: lettuce, Fresh Tomato Salsa, Chipotle Garlic Mayonnaise and a portion of fish. Serve with the lemon wedges to squeeze over.

FRIED TORTILLA WITH BLACK BEANS

SALSA VERDE
1–2 fresh green chillies/chiles, stems removed
2 garlic cloves, peeled
2–3 fresh tomatillos, husks removed (or canned tomatillos)
3 tablespoons chopped coriander/cilantro
¼ chopped onion
1 teaspoon rock salt

COOKED BLACK BEANS
175 g/1 cup dried black (turtle) beans
1 tablespoon vegetable oil
¼ onion, finely chopped
1 garlic clove, finely chopped
1 teaspoon ground avocado leaves
a pinch of sea salt

250 ml/1 cup vegetable oil
1 onion, cut into large chunks
1 large garlic clove, peeled and bruised
1 quantity Cooked Black Beans (see above)
12 corn tortillas

TO SERVE
200 g/2 cups crumbled feta cheese
1 head of Romaine lettuce, shredded
1 avocado, peeled, pitted and cut into strips
Salsa Verde (see above)

SERVES 4

MUCH OF THE JOY IN MEXICAN FOOD IS IN LOVED ONES GETTING TOGETHER AND TUCKING IN WITH THEIR HANDS, WHICH IS WHY STREET-STYLE FOOD IS SO POPULAR IN THIS PART OF THE WORLD!

Preheat the oven to 200°C (400°F) Gas 6.

For the Salsa Verde, put the chillies/chiles, garlic and tomatillos on a baking sheet and roast in the preheated oven for 20 minutes or until charred. If using canned tomatillos, don't roast them.

Halve the chillies and scoop out the seeds. Use a pestle and mortar to pound the chillies, garlic and salt into a paste. Add the tomatillos and pound until mixed. Stir in the coriander/cilantro and onion with a spoon. Add a little water or salt, if needed. Set aside.

Put the dried beans and 2 litres/8 cups water in a deep saucepan. Bring to a boil, then turn the heat down to low, partially cover and simmer gently for 2 hours. Check every 30 minutes to be sure there is still enough water and stir so that the beans don't stick to the pan.

After 2 hours, heat the oil in a large saucepan over medium heat and fry the onion, garlic and avocado leaves for 1 minute.

Add the beans and their cooking water and cook until the pan starts to boil, then turn the heat down to low, add the salt and cook for 10 minutes, crushing the beans regularly with a potato masher. Taste and add more salt if required. Put the cooked beans in a food processor and whizz for 3 minutes.

Heat 2 tablespoons of the oil in a frying pan/skillet over high heat, then fry the onion and garlic for about 5 minutes, until well browned. The onion and garlic are used only to flavour the oil, so remove them from the oil and discard.

Add the puréed beans to the pan, turn the heat down to low and simmer for 10 minutes. Remove from the heat and set aside to cool.

Put the remaining oil into a deep frying pan/skillet over medium heat. Heat until the oil is very hot but not smoking. Drop in a tortilla and cook for 15 seconds, then turn it over with tongs and cook for 1 minute, using a potato masher to hold the tortilla down flat in the oil.

Using the tongs or a slotted spoon, remove the tortilla from the pan and let drain on kitchen paper/paper towels. Repeat the process until all the tortillas have been fried.

To serve, put all fillings in bowls on a table for everyone to help themselves. Layer up the ingredients over the tortillas: beans, crumbled feta cheese, lettuce, avocado and Salsa Verde.

THOUGHT TO HAVE ITS ORIGIN IN THE OLYKEOK (OILY CAKE) – BROUGHT TO NEW YORK BY DUTCH SETTLERS – THE CLASSIC RING-SHAPED DOUGHNUT THAT WE KNOW AND LOVE TODAY IS ALL AMERICAN. HERE IS A FUN ALTERNATIVE FOR THE PERFECT BITE-SIZED SUGAR HIT.

DOUGHNUT POPCORN

100 ml/6½ tablespoons milk, warm

4 g/1¼ teaspoons fast-action dried/rapid-rise dry yeast

20 g/1½ tablespoons granulated sugar

150 g/1 cup plus 3 tablespoons all-purpose/plain flour, plus extra for dusting

80 g/²⁄₃ cup white bread/strong flour

½ teaspoon salt

1 egg, beaten

30 g/2 tablespoons butter, softened

1 teaspoon vanilla extract

sunflower oil, for greasing and frying

6 heaped tablespoons seedless raspberry jam/jelly

superfine/caster sugar, for dusting

2 baking sheets, lined with parchment paper and lightly dusted with flour

a piping bag with a round tip/nozzle

a small kitchen syringe (needle removed)

a 1¼-inch/3-cm round cookie cutter (optional)

paper popcorn cones, to serve (optional)

MAKES ABOUT 150 OR SERVES 6

Beat together the warm milk, yeast and sugar in a jug/pitcher and leave in a warm place for about 10 minutes until a thick foam has formed on top of the milk. Meanwhile, sift the flours into a large mixing bowl, add the salt, egg, butter and vanilla and stir together, then pour in the yeast mixture. Using a stand mixer fitted with a dough hook, mix the dough on a slow speed for 2 minutes, then increase the speed and knead for about 8 minutes until the dough is soft and pliable. Alternatively, knead the dough by hand for 15 minutes. The mixture will be very soft but should not be sticky, so dust with flour if needed.

Take very small pieces of dough, about the size of a bean, and roll into balls. The easiest way to do this is to roll the dough out and cut out 1¼-inch/3-cm circles using a round cutter, then cut each circle into quarters and roll each quarter into a ball. Place the balls on the prepared baking sheets and cover with a clean, damp tea/kitchen towel and let rest for 10 minutes, and then let rise in a warm place for about 35–45 minutes, covered in lightly-greased clingfilm/plastic wrap, until the dough has doubled in size and holds an indent when you press with a fingertip. Rest again, uncovered, for 10 minutes.

In a large saucepan or deep-fat fryer, heat the oil to 375°F (190°C). Holding the sheet of parchment, transfer the doughnuts to the oil, about 30 at a time, being careful not to handle the dough or splash hot oil. Cook for about 45 seconds on each side, gently turn over with tongs, until golden brown all over. Remove the doughnuts from the oil using a slotted spoon and drain on kitchen paper/paper towels.

Put the sugar on a plate and, when cool enough to handle, roll the doughnuts in it to coat. Spoon the jam/jelly into a piping bag and pipe into the syringe. Inject a small amount of jam/jelly into each doughnut, refilling the syringe using the piping bag, as necessary. Serve in popcorn cones, if using.

FRIED POTATOES ARE THE TYPE OF FOOD THAT TRANSCENDS CULTURAL BOUNDARIES, WITH MANY COUNTRIES HAVING THEIR OWN VERSIONS AND TRADITIONAL TOPPINGS. IN SPAIN, YOU HAVE PATATAS BRAVAS, A ONE-BOWL WONDER YOU'D EXPECT TO FIND IN EVERY SELECTION OF TAPAS- OR PINTXO-SELLING RESTAURANT OR BAR. HERE, THE CLASSIC RECIPE HAS BEEN GIVEN A LITTLE FACELIFT AS SWEET POTATOES AND CHERRY TOMATOES ARE USED.

PATATAS BRAVAS

2 large potatoes
2 orange-fleshed sweet potatoes
4 tablespoons olive oil
1 onion, chopped
2 garlic cloves, sliced
1 teaspoon coriander seeds
1 teaspoon cumin seeds
1 teaspoon Spanish smoked paprika
a big pinch of crushed dried chillies/
   chiles
150 g/5 oz. cherry tomatoes
sea salt and freshly ground black
   pepper
freshly chopped flat-leaf parsley,
   to garnish

SERVES 4

Preheat the oven to 225°C (425°F) Gas 7.

Peel and cut the large potatoes into large, bite-sized chunks, tip into a saucepan of salted water and bring to a boil. Cook over medium heat for about 5–7 minutes. Drain and leave the potatoes to dry in the colander.

Peel and cut the sweet potato into chunks the same size as the other potatoes and tip into a roasting dish. Add the blanched potatoes, drizzle half the olive oil over them and roast in the preheated oven for about 30 minutes, until lightly golden and tender.

Meanwhile, heat the remaining olive oil in a frying pan/skillet. Add the onion and cook for 2–3 minutes until tender but not coloured. Add the garlic and spices and cook for another 2 minutes until golden and fragrant. Add the cherry tomatoes to the pan and continue to cook until they start to soften.

Tip the contents of the pan into the roasting dish with the potatoes, season with salt and black pepper, stir to combine and return to the oven for another 5 minutes. Serve warm, garnished with the chopped parsley.

PIZZAS ARE PROBABLY ONE OF THE MOST ICONIC FAST FOODS TO HAVE COME
FROM ITALY. REGION TO REGION YOU'LL FIND VARIATIONS ON WHAT COUNTS AS
A 'CLASSIC' OR TRADITIONAL TOPPING. THESE MINI PIZZAS ARE A GREAT
CHANCE TO THROW CAUTION TO THE WIND AND DO WHAT TAKES YOUR FANCY.

PIZZETTES

BASE/CRUST
170 g/1½ cups plain/all-purpose
   or wholemeal/whole-wheat
   flour
a small pinch of fast-action
   dried/rapid-rise dry yeast
1 tablespoon olive oil
a pinch of sea salt
1 teaspoon caster/granulated
   sugar

TOPPING
1 tablespoon olive oil
300 g/1½ oz. pancetta, thinly
   sliced or diced
400-g/14-oz. can of tomatoes,
   drained and chopped
a big pinch of freshly chopped
   parsley
a big pinch of freshly chopped
   or dried oregano
1 tablespoon tomato purée/
   paste
about 40 g/1½ oz. caramelized
   red onions (optional)
200 g/7 oz. pecorino or
   Parmesan cheese, grated
   or shaved
sea salt and freshly ground
   black pepper

*a large baking sheet, greased or
lined with parchment paper*

MAKES 6

Preheat the oven to 180°C (350°F) Gas 4.

For the base/crust, put all the ingredients in a bowl,
add 125 ml/½ cup water and mix together with your hands
to make a dough. If the mixture feels sloppy, just add a little
more flour, or add a little more water for the opposite (it
shouldn't be so dry that it crumbles when you roll it). Turn
the dough out onto a flour-dusted surface and knead for
5–10 minutes, until smooth and elastic. The kneading can
be hard work but just remember that you need to do
it or your base will be chewy and tough. If you have a bread
maker, it will do the work for you – just follow the timing
instructions for your machine.

Divide the dough into six even pieces. On a flour-dusted
surface, roll out each into an oval. Place the now bases/crusts
on the prepared baking sheet and bake in the preheated
oven for 10 minutes, turning over halfway through.

Meanwhile, prepare the topping. Heat the olive oil
in a frying pan/skillet. Add the pancetta and fry over medium
heat, until fully cooked – let it brown but don't reduce it right
down at this stage because it will continue to bake on top of
the pizzettes. Put the canned tomatoes, parsley, oregano and
tomato purée/paste into a bowl, season with salt and
pepper, and mix well.

Once the pizza bases/crusts are initially baked, remove
from the oven. Spread the tomato mixture over the top
of the bases/crusts and then spoon over the caramelized
onions, if using. Put the pancetta pieces on top, then sprinkle
over the cheese.

Return the pizzettes to the preheated oven on the middle
shelf (ideally, put the pizzettes directly onto the oven shelf,
rather than using the baking sheet, so the bases can
continue to crisp) and bake for an additional 15 minutes,
until the cheese has melted. Serve hot.

THIS RECIPE IS A FANTASTIC WEINER SAUSAGE VERSION OF THE STAPLE SAUSAGE ROLL YOU'D OFTEN FIND FEATURED AS PARTY BUFFETS IN BRITISH HOMES, OR SOLD AT BAKERIES AS A TAKE-OUT SNACK.

SAUSAGE ROLLS

Put the yeast and water in the bowl of a stand mixer with a dough hook attached and mix until dissolved. If using active dried yeast, follow the instructions on the package – usually beat together the lukewarm liquid and yeast in a bowl and leave in a warm place for 15 minutes to activate and become frothy before using. Once activated, pour into the bowl of your stand mixer.

Add the sugar and stir again. Mix the salt into the flour and then, while mixing at a medium speed, start to add the flour – around half of it – and mix until well combined. Add the yogurt, oil and half of the beaten egg and keep mixing. Add more flour slowly, stopping when you have a mixture that starts to let go of the sides of the bowl. Be aware that you might not need all the flour.

Leave the dough to rise in a warm place, in a bowl covered with clingfilm/plastic wrap, for around 40 minutes, until doubled in size.

Roll the dough out on a lightly floured work surface, then split into two equal balls. Roll the first ball out into a circle of around 30 cm/11¾ inches in diameter, then use a pizza cutter to divide it into eight triangles. Brush each triangle with tomato ketchup (leaving the tip clear), then place a sausage piece at the thick end and roll up, like a croissant, with the sausage at the centre. Place on the prepared baking sheets with end of the fold underneath. Repeat for the rest of the sausages and dough. Leave the dough to rise for a final 15–20 minutes, then brush with the remaining beaten egg and scatter with sesame seeds.

Preheat the oven to 180°C (350°F) Gas 4.

Bake the sausage rolls in the preheated oven for around 15 minutes, until the dough is baked through and the rolls are golden.

25 g/1 oz. fresh yeast or 13 g/2½ teaspoons dried active/active dry yeast
250 ml/1 cup plus 1 tablespoon lukewarm water (35–37°C/97–98°F)
1 tablespoon sugar
1 teaspoon salt
400–500 g/14 oz.–1 lb. 2 oz. white/strong bread flour
100 g/½ cup minus ½ tablespoons plain yogurt
50 ml/3½ tablespoons olive or rapeseed oil

1 egg, beaten
500 g/1 lb. 2 oz. (roughly) wiener sausages cut into sixteen 6–7-cm/2½-inch pieces
good-quality tomato ketchup (or see page 22 for Homemade Tomato Ketchup)
white sesame seeds, to garnish

2 baking sheets, lined with parchment paper

Makes 16

A BRITISH CHIP SHOP MUST-HAVE, ESPECIALLY WHEN SEARCHING FOR SOME
SUSTENANCE AT THE END OF A BIG NIGHT OUT! THE SAUCE IS USUALLY A
POWDERED MIX, BUT WHEN HOMEMADE, IT ELEVATES THIS WELL ABOVE THE
AVERAGE. DEPENDING ON HOW HOT YOU LIKE YOUR CURRY, ADJUST THE
CURRY-POWDER HEAT IN THE RECIPE. GREAT WITH AN ICE-COLD LAGER.

CURRY CHIPS

CURRY SAUCE
2 tablespoons vegetable oil
1 onion, grated
1 apple, peeled and grated
1 garlic clove, crushed
2-cm/$3/4$-inch piece of fresh ginger,
  peeled and grated
2 tablespoons medium-hot curry
  powder
1 teaspoon turmeric
1 teaspoon paprika
2 teaspoons ground cumin
$1/2$ teaspoon ground coriander
1 tablespoon plain/all-purpose flour
500 ml/2 cups chicken or vegetable
  stock
1 teaspoon Worcestershire sauce
1 tablespoon tomato purée/paste
freshly squeezed lemon juice
  and/or sugar, to taste

CLASSIC CHIPS/FRIES
3–4 large floury potatoes,
  all roughly the same size
vegetable or sunflower oil
sea salt flakes

SERVES 4

First prepare the Curry Sauce. Heat the oil in a large non-stick
frying pan/skillet with the onion. Cook over a medium heat, stirring
occasionally, until aromatic, 3–5 minutes. Add the apple, garlic,
ginger, curry powder, turmeric, paprika, ground cumin and ground
coriander and cook, stirring for about 1 minute.

Add the flour, add a splash more oil if it is very dry, and cook,
stirring continuously for another 1 minute. While stirring, gradually
pour in the stock and stir until well blended. Bring just to a boil,
then lower the heat to a simmer. Stir in the Worcestershire sauce
and tomato purée/paste and simmer for 15 minutes. Taste. Depending
on preference, add some lemon juice for more acidity or a pinch
of sugar to sweeten, or both. Transfer to a blender and whizz until
smooth. Set aside.

Peel the potatoes and trim the sides to get a block. Cut the block
into slices about 1-cm/$3/8$-inch thick, then cut the slices again to get
chips/fries. Put the potatoes into a bowl of iced water for at least
5 minutes, to remove excess starch and prevent sticking when frying.

Fill a large saucepan one-third full with oil or, if using a deep-fat
fryer, follow the manufacturer's instructions. Heat the oil to 190°C
(375°F), until a cube of bread browns in 30 seconds.

Drain the potatoes and dry very well. Working in batches, fry
about a handful of potatoes at a time. Place the potatoes in a frying
basket (or use a slotted metal spoon) and lower into the hot oil
carefully. Fry for 4 minutes. Remove and drain on kitchen paper/
paper towels. Repeat until all of the potatoes have been fried.

Just before serving, skim any debris off the top of the cooking
oil and reheat to the same temperature.

Fry as before, in batches, but only cook until crisp and golden,
about 2 minutes. Remove and drain on kitchen paper/paper towels.
Repeat until all of the potatoes have been fried again. To serve,
reheat the Curry Sauce and pour over the chips/fries on a platter.

FISH AND CHIPS/FRIES MAKE MANY BRITISH PEOPLE FEEL NOSTALGIC. WHETHER IT BE MEMORIES OF MIDWEEK CHIP SHOP TAKEAWAYS OR WEEKEND TRIPS TO THE SEASIDE WHERE FISH AND CHIPS/FRIES WERE NON-NEGOTIABLE AS YOU WALKED ALONG THE SEA FRONT. THIS FANCY STREET-FOOD TAKE ON THE DISH HAS BREADED GOUJONS – PERFECT TO EAT WANDERING ALONG THE PROMENADE, OR WHEREVER THE WEATHER TAKES YOU. DRENCH THE CHUNKY CHIPS/FRIES IN SALT AND VINEGAR FOR A TRUE BRITISH EXPERIENCE.

SOLE GOUJONS & CHIPS

2 tablespoons olive oil
2 tablespoons unsalted butter
200 g/4 cups fresh, fine
   breadcrumbs
1 tablespoon freshly chopped
   flat-leaf parsley
2 teaspoons freshly chopped
   thyme
finely grated zest of 1 lemon
1 teaspoon Spanish smoked
   paprika
450 g/1 lb. skinless sole fillets
4 tablespoons plain/all-purpose
   flour
2 eggs, beaten
sea salt and freshly ground
   black pepper

TO SERVE
tomato ketchup (or see page
   22 for Homemade Tomato
   Ketchup)
tartar sauce
oven-cooked chips/fries (see
   page 47 for Classic Chips/
   Fries)
lemon wedges

a baking sheet, lined with
   parchment paper

SERVES 4

Preheat the oven to 220°C (425°F) Gas 7.

Heat the oil and butter in a large frying pan/skillet, add the breadcrumbs and, stirring constantly, cook until golden. Tip the crumbs into a large bowl, add the chopped herbs, lemon zest and paprika and season well with salt and black pepper. Let cool.

Cut each sole fillet into strips roughly 2–3 cm/1 inch wide. Tip the flour into one shallow dish and the beaten eggs into another. Taking one piece of fish at a time, coat it first in the flour, then the beaten eggs, then the golden breadcrumbs.

Arrange the goujons on the prepared baking sheet and bake in the preheated oven for about 10 minutes, until cooked through.

Serve immediately with tomato ketchup, tartar sauce, chips/fries and lemon wedges.

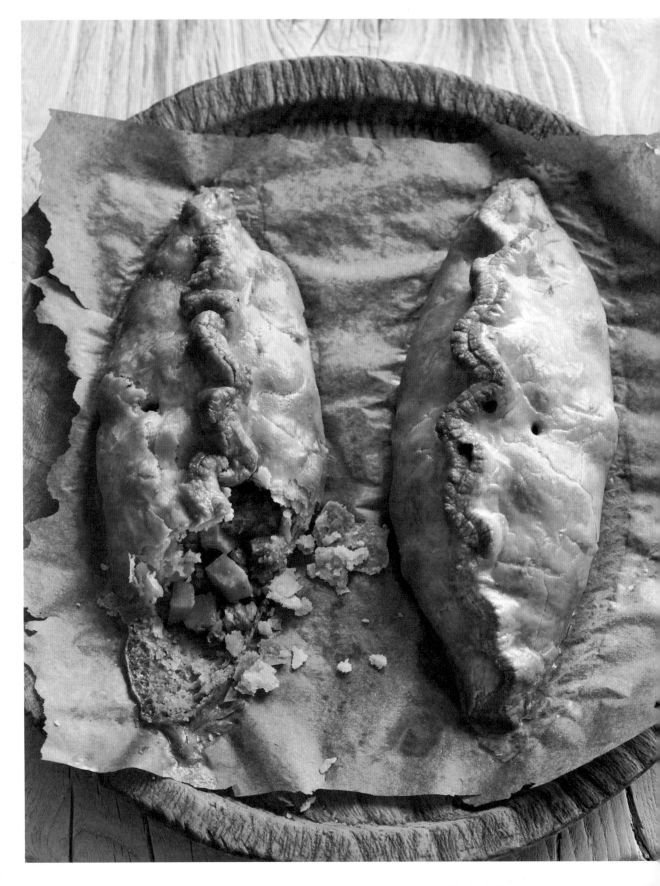

PASTIES ARE DELICIOUS HAND-HELD PIES MOST ASSOCIATED WITH THE UK'S SOUTHWESTERN COUNTIES OF DEVON AND CORNWALL. TRADITIONALLY MADE WITH A FILLING OF MEAT, POTATO AND VEGETABLES, THIS VERSION ISN'T TOO FAR FROM WHAT YOU'D FIND IN A LOCAL PASTRY SHOP. EATEN HOT OR COLD, THESE ARE PERFECT PICNIC OR PACKED-LUNCH FODDER, OR YOU COULD ALWAYS MAKE 12 MINI ONES FOR FANTASTIC, HOMELY CANAPÉS.

CORNED BEEF & SWEET POTATO PASTIES

SHORTCRUST PASTRY
250 g/2 cups plain/all-purpose flour
a pinch of salt
50 g/3 tablespoons lard (or white cooking fat/shortening), chilled and diced
75 g/5 tablespoons unsalted butter, chilled and diced
2 –3 tablespoons ice-cold water

FILLING
2 tablespoons sunflower oil
1 onion, finely chopped
1 large orange-fleshed sweet potato, diced
2 tablespoons spicy mango chutney or sweet chilli sauce
2 tablespoons chopped fresh thyme or lemon thyme
450 g/1 lb. canned corned beef, chilled and diced
1 egg, beaten, to glaze
salt and freshly ground black pepper

a 20-cm/8-inch dinner plate
a baking sheet, lined with parchment paper

MAKES 6

First, prepare the pastry. Sift the flour and salt together into a large mixing bowl. Add the lard and butter and rub together with your fingertips in until the mixture resembles breadcrumbs. Add enough of the water to bring the pastry together, and stir in to form a dough.

Tip onto a lightly floured surface and knead lightly to bring the dough together. Shape into a flattened ball, wrap in clingfilm/ plastic wrap and chill for at least 30 minutes before rolling out.

Once chilled, roll out the pastry on a lightly floured surface and cut out 6 rounds, using the plate as a guide.

Heat the oil in a frying pan/skillet and add the onion. Cook over medium heat for 5 minutes until beginning to soften. Add the sweet potato and cook, stirring from time to time, for 10 minutes or until just tender. Stir in the chutney or sweet chilli sauce and thyme and let cool. Once cold, mix in the corned beef and season well with salt and pepper.

Divide the mixture between the 6 pastry circles and crimp the edges together to seal in the filling – over the top or to the side, the choice is yours! Brush with the beaten egg and chill for 30 minutes.

Preheat the oven to 200°C (400°F) Gas 6.

Arrange the chilled pasties on the prepared baking sheet, make a little steam hole in each one and bake in the preheated oven for 20–30 minutes until the pastry is golden brown. Remove from the oven and serve hot or transfer to a wire rack to cool.

IN THE COASTAL REGIONS OF GREECE AND OTHER EASTERN MEDITERRANEAN COUNTRIES, THESE TINY DEEP-FRIED FISH ARE A POPULAR QUICK SNACK, ALONG WITH OTHER SEAFOOD FAVOURITES SUCH AS FRESH OYSTERS AND PRAWNS/SHRIMP – BEST EATEN FRESH WITH A SQUEEZE OF LEMON.

DEEP-FRIED WHITEBAIT WITH LEMON

500 g/1 lb. 2 oz. fresh whitebait
sunflower oil, for frying
4 tablespoons plain/all-purpose flour
1 scant teaspoon paprika
sea salt
a bunch of fresh flat-leaf parsley,
  finely chopped
1–2 lemons, cut into wedges

SERVES 4

Wash and drain the fish well – if they are fresh and tiny there is no need for any other preparation. However, if you have substituted with a slightly larger fish, you will need to scale and gut them.

Heat enough sunflower oil for deep frying in a heavy-bottomed pan. Combine the flour, paprika and salt and toss the whitebait in the mixture, coating them in the flour, but shake off any excess. Fry the fish in batches for 2–3 minutes, until crispy and golden. Drain on kitchen paper/paper towels.

Transfer the whitebait to a serving dish, sprinkle with salt and gently toss in the parsley. Serve with the lemon or with harissa.

WHEN IT COMES TO STREET-FOOD PAELLA, FOUND ALL ACROSS SPAIN, BIGGER ALWAYS SEEMS TO BE BETTER. WHEN PREPARED IN HUGE COOKING PANS, THIS TEMPTING DISH IS QUITE THE SPECTACLE TO PASSERS-BY!

CHICKEN & SEAFOOD PAELLA

500 g/1 lb. 2 oz. fresh mussels, cleaned
100 ml/¹⁄₃ cup dry white wine
8 large prawns/jumbo shrimp
8 langoustines (optional)
¹⁄₄ teaspoon saffron strands
6 tablespoons olive oil
4 skinless chicken thigh fillets, quartered
350 g/12 oz. prepared squid rings
4 large garlic cloves, crushed
1 red (bell) pepper, seeded and chopped
2 tomatoes, finely chopped
1 teaspoon sweet paprika
350 g/scant 2 cups bomba, Calasparra or Arborio rice
200 g/1¹⁄₃ cups fresh or frozen peas
salt and freshly ground black pepper
freshly chopped parsley, to garnish

Serves 4

Discard any mussels that do not close when tapped on the work surface. Place the mussels, still wet from cleaning, in a saucepan and place over a medium heat. Add the wine and cook the mussels, covered, for 4–5 minutes, until the shells have opened (discard any that remain closed). Strain and reserve the liquid. Set the mussels aside.

Remove the heads from the prawns/shrimp and langoustines and add the heads to the mussel liquid along with 1.25 litres/5 cups cold water. Bring to a boil, skimming the surface to remove any scum, and simmer gently for 30 minutes. Strain the stock through a fine sieve/strainer into a saucepan (you should have about 1 litre/generous 4 cups), stir in the saffron strands and keep warm.

Heat half the oil in a 35-cm/14-inch paella pan (or shallow flameproof casserole dish) and fry the chicken pieces for about 5 minutes, until browned. Remove with a slotted spoon and set aside. Repeat with the prawns/shrimp, and then the langoustines, if using, and finally the squid rings, frying for 2–3 minutes, until golden, removing each with a slotted spoon.

Reduce the heat, add the remaining oil to the pan and gently fry the garlic for 5 minutes until softened. Stir in the pepper, tomatoes and paprika, and cook for about 5 minutes, until the sauce is sticky. Stir in the rice and return the chicken to the pan. Add the stock, bring to a boil and simmer gently for 10 minutes.

Stir in the prawns/shrimp, langoustines, mussels, squid and peas, and cook for an additional 10 minutes, until the rice and seafood are cooked. Season to taste, then let rest for 10 minutes before serving, sprinkled with chopped parsley.

IF EVER THERE WAS A CHEESE THAT IMPROVES WITH COOKING, IT'S HALLOUMI, SO IT'S NO WONDER IT WORKS FANTASTICALLY WELL AS CRISPY FRIES. HALLOUMI HAILS FROM THE MIDDLE EAST, BUT THIS 'FRIES' TAKE ON THE GREEK FRIED CHEESE, *HORS D'OEUVRE SAGANAKI*, IS AN ENTIRELY BRITISH CREATION. ENJOY THESE SALTY, SQUEAKY STICKS WITH A RICH BEETROOT, YOGURT & MINT DIP, OR ROLL IT ALL UP IN FLATBREAD WITH SOME CRISP LETTUCE.

HALLOUMI & ZA'ATAR FRIES

BEETROOT/BEETS, YOGURT & MINT DIP
400 g/14 oz. cooked beetroot/beets
2 tablespoons extra virgin olive oil
6–8 tablespoons Greek yogurt
2 garlic cloves, crushed
pinch of ground cumin
few fresh mint leaves, finely chopped
salt and freshly ground black pepper
400 g/14 oz. halloumi

150 g/1 cup plus 1 tablespoon plain/all-purpose flour
1 tablespoons za'atar spice mix, plus more to serve
vegetable oil
lemon wedges, to serve
Beetroot/Beets, Yogurt & Mint Dip (see left), to serve

Serves 2–4 as a side

For the Beetroot/Beets, Yogurt & Mint Dip, combine the beetroot/beets, oil and yogurt in a food processor or blender and whizz to obtain a coarse dip. Transfer to a bowl and stir in the garlic, cumin and a pinch of salt. Taste and adjust seasoning. Sprinkle with the mint and set aside.

Cut the halloumi into 2-cm/3/4-inch wide strips.

Combine the flour and za'atar in a shallow bowl and mix well.

Fill a large saucepan one-third full with the oil or, if using a deep-fat fryer, follow the manufacturer's instructions. Heat the oil to 190°C (375°F), until a cube of bread browns in 30 seconds.

Working in batches, coat the halloumi strips in the flour mixture. Place in a frying basket and lower into the hot oil carefully. Fry until golden, for 3–4 minutes. Remove and drain on kitchen paper/paper towels. Repeat until all of the halloumi has been fried.

To serve, mound the fries on a platter and scatter over some za'atar. Serve with lemon wedges and the Beetroot/Beets Yogurt and Mint Dip.

FILO/PHYLLO PASTRY IS WIDELY USED IN GREEK COOKERY - IT CAN BE FRIED
OR OVEN-BAKED AND COOKS VERY QUICKLY, IDEAL FOR HUNGRY CUSTOMERS
QUEUEING UP FOR A TASTY LUNCH-TIME SNACK! HERE, WAFER-THIN LAYERS
CONCEAL A SWEET AND MOIST MEAT, DATE AND CRANBERRY FILLING.

FILLED CRISPY FILO ROLLS

olive oil, for frying
1 small onion, finely diced
250 g/9 oz. minced/ground lamb
150 g/5½ oz. minced/ground pork
2 generous pinches of ground
   cinnamon
a generous pinch of smoked paprika
a pinch of ground cumin
a small pinch of ground cloves
2 tablespoons sunflower seeds
2 tablespoons diced pitted dates
2 tablespoons dried cranberries
2 tablespoons Greek dried oregano
½ tablespoon cornflour/cornstarch
100 ml/⅓ cup cold water
a handful of fresh flat-leaf parsley,
   chopped
a handful of fresh mint, chopped
12 sheets filo/phyllo pastry (25 x 15 cm/
   10 x 6 inches), see Note, at the
   bottom of the method
50 g/3½ tablespoons butter, melted
1 tablespoon fennel seeds
a pinch of dried chilli/hot red pepper
   flakes
a pinch of salt
tzatziki, to serve

*a baking sheet, lined with parchment
   paper*

MAKES ABOUT 12

Preheat the oven to 180°C (360°F) Gas 4.

Heat a drizzle of olive oil in a pan, add the onion and fry until
soft and translucent, but don't let it brown. Add the lamb and pork,
spices, seeds, dates, cranberries and oregano, and cook until the
meat is well browned and any residual juices have evaporated.

Make a paste with the cornflour and cold water and pour into
the pan. Heat until the water bubbles – this is just to loosen the
mixture slightly; it will evaporate quickly. Remove from the heat
and add the parsley and mint.

Lay out a sheet of filo/phyllo in front of you lengthways and
lightly brush the surface with melted butter. Place a couple of
tablespoons of the meat mixture in the middle, about 2.5 cm/1 inch
from the bottom. Roll the pastry over once, then fold in the edges
(encasing the mixture) and roll to the end.

You want quite thick, chunky rolls, so make sure you put plenty
of filling in. Once you've given it a full roll, you can trim the end if
need be; you don't want too much pastry. Place seam-side down on
the lined baking sheet. Repeat with the remaining pastry and filling.
Lightly butter the top of each roll and sprinkle fennel seeds, chilli
flakes and salt over the top.

Bake in the preheated oven for 10 minutes, until the outside
shell has crisped and turned slightly golden. These go well with
a little tzatziki and a cold beer.

Note: Filo/phyllo pastry is wafer thin and dries out quickly
once unwrapped, so you need to work quickly. If you take longer
than even just a few minutes to shape your filo/phyllo rolls, it will
dry out, turn brittle and be impossible to work with! Each time
you remove a sheet of it, either roll the rest back up, or cover with
a damp tea/kitchen towel to keep it moist.

POTATO CROQUETTES

4 medium-sized old variety potatoes
(i.e. King Edward, Pentland Crown,
Maris Piper, Rooster), cleaned
½ teaspoon nutmeg
75 g/5 tablespoons unsalted butter
a generous handful of flat-leaf
parsley, freshly chopped
2 UK large/US extra large eggs, beaten
150 g/1¼ cups dried breadcrumbs
olive oil, for deep frying
sea salt and freshly ground black
pepper
Fried Courgette/Zucchini Flowers,
to serve (see Note)

a baking sheet, lined with parchment
paper

SERVES 4–6

Place the potatoes in a saucepan of boiling water. Keep the potatoes cooking but not boiling. Cook for about 15 minutes, until tender.

When the potatoes are tender, drain and let cool. Peel away the skins and press the potatoes through a ricer or food mill into a bowl. Don't use a food processor as this will develop the starch too much.

Add the nutmeg, butter, parsley and salt and pepper. Mix well and form into 10 x 7.5-cm/4 x 3-inch pieces, rolled into small rods.

Dip the rods into the beaten egg, then the breadcrumbs. Place on the prepared baking sheet and chill in the fridge for 30 minutes.

Heat the oil and fry in batches until golden. Drain on kitchen paper/paper towels and sprinkle over some more salt. Serve hot.

Note: For the Fried Cougette/Zucchini Flowers, dissolve 7 g/ 1¼ teaspoons fresh yeast in a little warm water. Set aside for 10 minutes. Mix together 250 g/2 cups Italian 'oo' flour, 450 ml/ 1¾ cups warm water, 2 tablespoons olive oil, yeast mixture and salt and pepper. Cover and leave for 45–60 minutes. Stir the bubbles in the batter. Heat 8 cm/3 inches of groundnut oil in a deep pan. Remove the stamens from 24 courgette/zucchini flowers. Dip the flowers into the batter and shake off the excess. Place one at a time in the oil, frying 4 at a time until golden, turning once. Remove with a slotted spoon and drain on kitchen paper/paper towels, then sprinkle with parsley and salt and serve with lemon quarters, to squeeze over.

THE HUMBLE SANDWICH IS SURELY ONE OF THE MOST MOBILE FOODS OF THEM ALL – DELICIOUS BREAD HOLDING ANY TYPE OF FILLING YOU CAN THINK OF. THIS VERSION, THE OPEN SANDWICH, IS A NORDIC LUNCHTIME STAPLE – IN CITY CENTRES YOU WON'T BE FAR FROM BEING ABLE TO GRAB ONE (OR TWO!) FROM A TAKE-OUT STALL OR BAKERY. HERE ARE TWO VERSIONS: A CLASSIC HERRING, AND ANOTHER FOR THOSE WHO DON'T LIKE STRONG-TASTING FISH!

NORDIC OPEN SANDWICHES

HERRING
150 g/5 oz. new potatoes
150 g/5 oz. mustard herring, diced
5 tablespoons mayonnaise
a small handful fresh dill, finely
    chopped
6 slices of archipelago or rye bread

MAKES 6

For the Herring open sandwich, boil the potatoes until cooked through, then drain and let cool. Peel off the skin and dice the flesh.

Mix the chopped potatoes, herring, mayonnaise and dill together in a small bowl. There is no need to season, as the herring is already full of flavour. Spread the mixture on top of the slices of bread.

SUMMER SALAD

200 g/6 oz. new potatoes
¼ small onion, diced
⅓ cucumber, diced
2 tablespoons white wine vinegar
150 ml sour/soured cream
3 halves of a rye baguette
sea salt and freshly ground black
** pepper**

MAKES 3

For the Summer Salad open sandwich, boil the potatoes until cooked through, then drain and let cool. Peel off the skin and dice the flesh.

Mix the chopped potatoes, onion and cucumber together in a small bowl. Put the vinegar and sour/soured cream in a separate bowl and stir to combine. Add salt and black pepper to taste, then stir into the chopped potato mixture. Spread the mixture on top of the baguette halves.

THERE ARE MANY REGIONAL DUMPLING RECIPES IN THIS BOOK AND PIEROGI IS THE MUCH-LOVED POLISH VERSION – HERE IS A SAVOURY RECIPE WITH CHIVES ADDED TO A CLASSIC POTATO AND CHEESE FILLING, WHICH GIVES THEM A LITTLE LIFT!

POTATO, CHEESE & CHIVE PIEROGI

350 g/2²/₃ cups plain/all-purpose
  flour, plus extra for dusting
1 teaspoon salt
1 egg, beaten
1 tablespoon vegetable
  or sunflower oil
250 ml/1 cup plus 1 tablespoon
  warm water

POTATO FILLING
225 g/8 oz. floury potatoes,
  peeled and chopped
500 g/1 lb 2 oz. cottage cheese
20 g/³/₄ oz. chives, finely
  chopped
freshly grated nutmeg
salt and freshly ground pepper

TO SERVE
25 g/1¹/₂ tablespoons butter, for
  frying
2–3 tablespoons sour/soured
  cream
paprika, for sprinkling

a 8-cm/3¹/₄-inch circular pastry
  cutter

MAKES ABOUT 30

First, make the dough. Sift the flour into a bowl and stir in the salt. Make a well in the centre and add in the egg and oil. Using your fingers, mix the flour with the egg and oil and gradually add and work in the warm water until the mixture comes together to form a soft, sticky dough.

Place the dough on a floured surface and knead well for around 8–10 minutes until smooth and supple. Cover the dough with a clean tea/kitchen towel and chill in the fridge for 1 hour or overnight.

Meanwhile, for the filling, cook the potatoes in boiling, salted water until tender; drain and mash. Set aside to cool. Just before you begin rolling out the dough, mix together the mashed potato, cottage cheese and chives (reserving a tablespoon for garnish). Season with freshly grated nutmeg, salt and freshly ground black pepper.

Thinly roll out the dough on a well-floured surface to a thickness of around 3 mm/¹/₈ inch. Using the circular cutter, cut out rounds from it. To make each pierogi, place a heaped teaspoon of the filling mixture on one half of a dough circle and fold over the dough, pressing and pinching together to seal it well. Place each pierogi spaced well apart (so as not to stick together) on a floured surface. Bring a large pot of salted water to the boil and cook the pierogi in batches. Gently add in a few pierogi at a time, so as not to overcrowd the pan, and cook for around 2–3 minutes until they float to the surface. Carefully remove them with a slotted spoon and set aside.

Repeat the process until all the pierogi have been cooked.

Melt the butter in a large frying pan/skillet. Add in the pierogi and fry for a few minutes on each side until lightly golden brown. Serve the fried pierogi at once, with sour/soured cream, and garnish with paprika, freshly ground black pepper and the reserved chopped chives.

Bulgarian bread is simply astonishing for its quality and variety, and this example, layered with feta cheese is just delicious.

BULGARIAN CHEESE BREAD

450 g/3²/₃ cups plain/all-
purpose white wheat flour
2 g/1¹/₈ teaspoons easy-bake dry
yeast, 4.5 g/1¹/₂ teaspoons
dried active/active dry yeast,
or 9 g/0.3 oz fresh yeast
250 g/1 cup milk, heated to
just below boiling point, then
cooled to room temperature
9 g/2¹/₄ teaspoons salt
100 g/6¹/₂ tablespoons butter

FILLING
1 egg
250 g/8 oz feta cheese,
crumbled into little pieces
50 g/3 tablespoons butter
paprika, freshly ground pepper
or chopped fresh herbs
of your choice (optional)

GLAZE
1 egg
1 teaspoon water

DECORATION
sprinkle of paprika (optional)

a 12 x 12-cm/4¹/₂ x 4¹/₂-inch
baking pan, at least 5 cm/
2 inches deep, greased
and lined with parchment
paper

MAKES 1 12 x 12-CM/4¹/₂ x 4¹/₂-
INCH LOAF OR 9 SQUARES

Put the flour into a bowl and make a well. Sprinkle the yeast in the well and pour on the milk. Close the well by flicking flour on the surface of the milk and allow it to rest for 1 hour.

Add the salt and gather everything into a ball in the bowl. Turn it out on the counter and knead for 10 minutes. Add the butter and knead for another 10 minutes. Pop the dough back in the bowl, cover and let rest for 2 hours.

Mix the egg for the filling together with the feta cheese in a bowl. Melt the butter and let cool.

Put the dough onto an unfloured surface. Shape the dough into a tight sausage. Cut it into 9 equal pieces. Lightly flour the top of each piece and let rest for 15 minutes under a dry tea/kitchen towel.

Take out one piece and, on a floury surface, roll it into a rectangle about 10 x 10 cm/4 x 4 inches. Brush it with the melted butter. Take out another piece, roll it into a rectangle the same size as before, place it on the first piece and brush it with melted butter. Take out a third piece, roll it into a rectangle the same size as before and place it on the stack. Don't brush it! Using a rolling pin, roll the stack of dough into a rectangle the size of your baking pan and lift it up and place it in the prepared baking pan. Brush it with melted butter and spread over half the feta cheese mixture and any optional toppings.

Repeat with the next 3 pieces of dough, and place that stack on top of the first stack. Brush this with melted butter and spread it with the other half of the feta cheese mixture and some more optional toppings.

Repeat with the final 3 pieces of dough, and place that stack on top of the dough in the pan.

With your hands, push down all around the outside edge of the stack of dough – between the dough and the pan – so that you seal in the cheese. Cover with a dry tea/kitchen towel and let rest for 1 hour.

Preheat the oven to 230°C (450°F) Gas 8.

Before baking, brush the top of the dough with melted butter and sprinkle some paprika on it if you like. Put the pan in the preheated oven and turn the oven down to 200°C (400°F) Gas 6. Bake for 35 minutes.

Remove from the oven. Transfer carefully to a wire rack and let cool a bit. While still warm, transfer the loaf to chopping board, cut it into squares and eat it alongside a salad or soup for a wonderful meal.

A CROSS BETWEEN A PANCAKE AND A FLATBREAD, SOCCA ARE MADE FROM GRAM/CHICKPEA FLOUR, OLIVE OIL AND WATER, AND HAIL FROM NICE IN THE SOUTH OF FRANCE WHERE YOU WILL SEE THEM BEING SOLD STRAIGHT FROM THE OVEN. NATURALLY WHEAT- AND GLUTEN-FREE, YOU CAN TOP THEM WITH ALMOST ANYTHING, BUT THIS RECIPE OF CHOPPED PARSLEY, OLIVES AND RED ONION WORKS WONDERFULLY WELL.

SOCCA

SOCCA
150 g/1 cup plus 2 tablespoons gram/chickpea flour
½ teaspoon salt
½ teaspoon ground turmeric
3 tablespoons olive oil
sunflower oil, for frying

TOPPING
handful of pitted black and green olives, chopped into small chunks
2 tablespoons freshly chopped parsley
1 red onion, very finely chopped
sea salt and freshly ground black pepper, to season
extra virgin olive oil, for drizzling
1 lemon

a 20-cm/8-inch non-stick frying pan/skillet

SERVES 6

To make the socca, sift the gram/chickpea flour into a bowl and add the salt and turmeric. Slowly add 380 ml/1²/₃ cups water, beating quickly all the time until all the water has been added, breaking up any lumps of flour as you go. Add 3 tablespoons olive oil and stir.

Heat a little sunflower oil in the non-stick frying pan/skillet until hot. Pour a ladleful of the batter into the pan, swirling it so that the mixture spreads to the edges. Reduce the heat to low–medium and cook gently. It will take a good 6–8 minutes on the first side. Resist the temptation to stick your spatula underneath it until the edges have completely dried out and the middle has tiny little bubbles. At this point, take the pan and shake from side to side. The pancake should move but if it is sticking you can help it along gently with a spatula. However, if it is not budging at all, leave it for another minute and then try again. Flip the pancake and cook for an additional 1 or 2 minutes. The second side does not need to be cooked for as long, as it is nice if it is still a little soft.

Repeat until all the batter has been used up, wrapping the pancakes in parchment paper and keeping warm in a low oven.

For the topping, liberally scatter the chopped olives, parsley and onion over the pancakes. Season with a good pinch of salt and pepper, a drizzle of olive oil and a squeeze of lemon juice.

To serve, cut the pancakes into wedges, as they do in the south of France, or roll them up into big cigars.

THESE CRISPY FRIED CHURROS ARE A VARIETY OF DOUGHNUT MOST POPULAR IN SPAIN AND ARE OFTEN SOLD IN PAPER CUPS WITH A POT OF MELTED CHOCOLATE SAUCE WEDGED INSIDE. GO TO A STREET-SIDE CAFÉ AND YOU MIGHT BE LUCKY ENOUGH TO HAVE THEM PAIRED WITH A WHOLE COFFEE MUG OF WARM CHOCOLATELY GOODNESS. DELICIOSO!

CHURROS WITH HOT CHOCOLATE SAUCE

300 g/3⅓ cups
    self-raising/rising
    flour
1 teaspoon baking
    powder
70 g ⅓ cup sugar
¼ teaspoon salt
2 eggs, beaten
grated zest of
    2 mandarins
2 teaspoons ground
    cinnamon
50 g/3 tablespoons
    butter, softened
1 teaspoon vanilla
    extract
250 ml/1 cup natural/
    plain yogurt
sunflower oil, for
    frying

CINNAMON SUGAR
120 g/²⁄₃ cup sugar

2 teaspoons ground
    cinnamon

HOT CHOCOLATE
    SAUCE
100 g/3½ oz. spiced
    dark chocolate (such
    as Aztec or Maya
    Gold)
100 g/3½ oz. milk
    chocolate
250 ml/1 cup milk
1 cinnamon stick
a pinch of red chilli/
    chili powder

*a piping bag fitted
    with a large star tip/
    nozzle*

MAKES 24

Sift the flour into a large mixing bowl. Add all the remaining ingredients (except the frying oil) and beat to a smooth batter with an electric hand mixer. Spoon the batter into the piping bag.

Fill a large saucepan or deep-fat fryer 10 cm/4 inches deep with oil and heat it to 350°F (180°C). Pipe the mixture into the pan in lengths of about 10 cm/4 inches, holding the piping bag in one hand and scissors in the other. Use the scissors to cut the dough at the desired length, being careful not to splash hot oil. Fry the churros in batches of five, cooking for about 5 minutes and turning frequently until golden brown all over. Remove one churros from the oil and cut it open to ensure the cake dough is cooked all the way through. When satisfied they are cooked, remove the churros from the oil using a slotted spoon and drain on kitchen paper/paper towels.

Put the cinnamon and sugar on a plate and mix together. Toss the warm churros in the sugar mixture to coat evenly.

For the hot chocolate sauce, put the chocolate, milk, cinnamon stick and chilli/chili in a saucepan and heat gently until the chocolate has melted. Remove the cinnamon stick, pour into a serving bowl and serve with the churros.

IN A WAFER CONE, A PAPER CUP OR MELTING DOWN YOUR CHIN AND FINGERS, ICE CREAM OR GELATO IS A SUMPTUOUS MUST-HAVE ON A WARM SUMMER'S DAY. WALK THE STREETS OF ITALY AND YOU'LL FIND ALL KINDS OF FRESH AND VIBRANT FLAVOURS. INTERESTINGLY, THE BRONTE PISTACHIO HAS BEEN GRANTED DOP (PROTECTED DESIGNATION OF ORIGIN) STATUS IN SICILY – PROVING IT TO BE THE VERY BEST. IF YOU CAN, GET YOUR HANDS ON THEM FOR THIS CLASSIC RECIPE.

PISTACHIO ICE CREAM

100 g/1 cup shelled pistachios, unsalted

450 ml/1³⁄₄ cups whole milk

450 ml/2 cups double/ heavy cream

1 teaspoon pure vanilla extract

¼ teaspoon sea salt, crushed

100 g/¹⁄₂ cup golden caster/granulated sugar

4 UK large/US extra large eggs

a baking sheet, lined with parchment paper
an ice cream maker

SERVES 4–6

Preheat the oven to 180°C (350°F) Gas 4.

On the baking sheet, spread the nuts out in a single layer and toast in the oven for 8 minutes. Remove and let cool.

Heat the milk and cream together in a saucepan until scalding.

Reserve some of the cooled nuts to decorate, then grind the rest in a food processor until fine but with a little texture, if you like. Add the vanilla and salt, and stir well.

Beat the sugar and eggs together until thick and creamy and the balloon/wire whisk leaves a trail when lifted from the bowl, approximately 8–10 minutes.

Combine the milk and egg mix together in the pan and gently cook this custard mixture over low heat. This should not take longer than 8 minutes. Stir really well to prevent it from scrambling.

If you would like a pronounced green ice cream, cool the mixture and leave overnight in the fridge, then freeze and churn in an ice cream maker as per the manufacturer's instructions. If you want your ice cream sooner rather than later, let the creamy pistachio custard cool, then freeze and churn.

Serve on its own, sprinkle the reserved nuts on top or with chocolate ice cream – they are rather good together.

FLAVOURS OF AFRICA
& THE MIDDLE EAST

WHEN MOST PEOPLE THINK OF HUMMUS, THEY THINK OF A THICK ROOM-TEMPERATURE PURÉE, NOT THIS DELECTABLE, TRADITIONAL HOT DISH. ITS ORIGIN IS CLAIMED BY MANY MIDDLE EASTERN COUNTIRES, EVEN EGYPT, WHERE A SIMILAR RECIPE APPEARS IN A THIRTEENTH-CENTURY COOKBOOK!

HOT HUMMUS WITH PINE NUTS & CHILLI BUTTER

2 x 400 g/14-oz. cans chickpeas, drained and thoroughly rinsed
2 teaspoons cumin seeds
2–3 garlic cloves, crushed
roughly 4 tablespoons olive oil
freshly squeezed juice of 2 lemons
2 tablespoons tahini
500 ml/2 cups natural/plain yogurt
sea salt and freshly ground black pepper
2 tablespoons pine nuts
50 g/3 tablespoons butter
1 teaspoon finely chopped dried red chilli/chile
warm crusty bread, to serve

SERVES 4–6

Preheat the oven to 200°C(400°F) Gas 6.

Tip the chickpeas into an electric blender. Add the cumin seeds, garlic, olive oil and lemon juice and whizz into a thick paste. Add the tahini and continue to blend until the mixture is really thick and smooth. Add the yogurt and whizz until the mixture has loosened a little and the texture is creamy. Season generously with salt and pepper and tip the mixture into an ovenproof dish.

Roast the pine nuts in small frying pan/skillet until they begin to brown and emit a nutty aroma. Add the butter to the pine nuts and stir until it melts. Stir in the chopped chilli/chile and pour the melted butter over the hummus, spooning the pine nuts all over the surface.

Pop the dish into the preheated oven for about 25 minutes, until the hummus has risen a little and most of the butter has been absorbed. Serve immediately with chunks of warm crusty bread.

TRADITIONAL CHICKPEA FALAFEL POCKETS

FALAFEL IS A POPULAR MIDDLE EASTERN SNACK MADE WITH CHICKPEAS. ALTHOUGH THE FALAFEL BITES ARE DEEP FRIED, THEY ARE LOW IN FAT, FILLING AND DELICIOUS SERVED WITH VEGETABLES IN A PITTA POCKET. PLAN AHEAD BECAUSE YOU WILL NEED TO SOAK THE CHICKPEAS FOR 12 HOURS BEFORE MAKING THE FALAFEL.

To make the Tahini Sauce, mix together the tahini paste, garlic, chives, lemon juice and a little salt and pepper, adding just enough milk to get a smooth sauce. Refrigerate any leftovers for later use.

For the falafels, soak the chickpeas in plenty of water for 12 hours. Drain, discarding the water, cover with fresh water and let soak for another 12 hours. Drain, rinse well and let drain again for another 5 minutes.

It's best to use a food processor fitted with an 'S' blade for blending the falafel mix, but it can also be done in a good blender, in two batches. First blend the drained chickpeas; the texture should resemble coarse sand. Add all the remaining ingredients (except the frying oil) and blend until you get a paste. Cover with clingfilm/plastic wrap and let sit in the fridge for 1 hour, or longer.

Roll into large walnut-sized balls, wetting your hands once in a while to prevent sticking.

Deep-fry the falafels in hot oil for 4 minutes, until nicely browned. Because the chickpeas are soaked and not canned, these falafels need to be deep-fried to make them digestible – baking them wouldn't work.

Warm the pitta pockets, fill with vegetables of your choice, falafel balls and drizzle with the tahini sauce.

TAHINI SAUCE
4 tablespoons tahini
1 garlic clove, crushed
1 tablespoon freshly snipped chives
freshly squeezed lemon juice, to taste
about 120 ml/½ cup oat, rice or almond milk
salt and freshly ground black pepper

180 g/1 cup dried chickpeas
80 g/²/₃ cup chopped onion
2 garlic cloves
1 bunch fresh parsley, leaves only
2 teaspoons ground coriander
½ teaspoon bicarbonate of soda/baking soda
1 teaspoon ground cumin
⅛ teaspoon chilli/chili powder
1½ teaspoons salt
230 ml/1 cup oil, for frying

TO SERVE
6 pitta pockets
Tahini Sauce (see left)
raw vegetables (such as sliced tomatoes, cucumber, lettuce, rocket/arugula, parsley, spring onions/scallions)

MAKES 24–26

FRESHLY CAUGHT MUSSELS ARE SHELLED, DIPPED IN BATTER AND FRIED IN A HUGE, CURVED PAN, SIMILAR TO A LARGE WOK, AND ARE SOLD IN THE PORTS OF ISTANBUL, IZMIR AND BEIRUT, AND AS CLASSIC MEZZE IN OTHER COASTAL REGIONS. THE JUICY, CRISPY-COATED MUSSELS ARE OFTEN PUSHED ONTO STICKS AND SERVED WITH A NUT SAUCE OR GARLICKY BREAD. THE SAME IDEA CAN BE APPLIED TO FRESH, SHELLED PRAWNS/SHRIMP OR STRIPS OF SQUID.

DEEP-FRIED MUSSELS IN BEER BATTER WITH GARLICKY WALNUT SAUCE

100 g/³/₄ cup plain/all-purpose flour
1 teaspoon salt
¹/₂ teaspoon bicarbonate of/ baking soda
2 egg yolks
150 ml/²/₃ cup light beer
sunflower oil, for deep frying
20 fresh, shelled mussels, thoroughly cleaned

NUT SAUCE
100 g/³/₄ cup walnuts
2 small slices day-old white bread, with crusts removed, soaked in a little water and squeezed dry
2 garlic cloves, crushed
3 tablespoons olive oil
freshly squeezed juice of 1 lemon
1 teaspoon runny honey
a dash of white wine vinegar
salt and freshly ground black pepper

wooden skewers, soaked in water

SERVES 4

To make the batter, sift the flour, salt and bicarbonate of/baking soda into a bowl. Make a well in the middle and drop in the egg yolks. Gradually pour in the beer, using a wooden spoon to draw in the flour from the sides. Beat well until thick and smooth. Put aside for 30 minutes.

Meanwhile, make the sauce. Using a pestle and mortar, pound the walnuts to a paste, or whizz them in an electric blender. Add the bread and garlic and pound to a paste. Drizzle in the olive oil, stirring all the time, and beat in the lemon juice and honey. Add the dash of vinegar and season well with salt and pepper (the sauce should be creamy, so add more olive oil or a little water if it is too thick). Spoon the sauce into a serving bowl.

Heat enough oil for deep frying in a shallow pan or a wok. Dip each mussel into the batter and drop them into the oil. Fry them in batches until golden brown and drain on kitchen paper/paper towels.

Thread the mussels onto small wooden skewers and serve immediately with the sauce for dipping.

MEATBALLS ARE EATEN DAILY IN THE MIDDLE EAST
AS MEZZE, STREET FOOD OR EVEN AS PART OF A MAIN
COURSE – THERE ARE SO MANY TYPES YOU CAN LOSE
COUNT, BUT THEY ARE MAINLY PREPARED FROM MINCED/
GROUND LAMB OR BEEF AND, SOMETIMES, MINCED/
GROUND CHICKEN OR FLAKED FISH. THESE MINI ONES,
CALLED 'CIZBIZ', ARE PERFECTLY BITE-SIZED AND
CONTAIN ROASTED PISTACHIOS IN THE MIDDLE AND
SERVED WITH WEDGES OF LEMON TO SQUEEZE OVER.

MINI MEATBALLS STUFFED WITH ROASTED PISTACHIOS

2–3 tablespoons pistachios,
    shelled
250 g/9 oz. lean minced/ground
    lamb
1 onion, finely chopped
2 garlic cloves, crushed
2 teaspoons ground cinnamon
a small bunch of fresh flat-leaf
    parsley, finely chopped
sea salt and freshly ground
    black pepper
sunflower oil
1–2 lemons, cut into wedges

SERVES 4–6

In a small heavy-bottomed pan, roast the pistachios for 1–2 minutes,
until they emit a nutty aroma. Using a pestle and mortar, crush most
of them lightly to break them into small pieces.

In a bowl, pound the minced/ground lamb with the onion, garlic
and cinnamon. Knead the mixture with your hands and slap it down
into the base of the bowl to knock out the air. Add the parsley and
seasoning and knead well to make sure it is thoroughly mixed.

Take cherry-sized portions of the mixture in your hands and roll
them into balls. Indent each ball with your finger, right into the middle,
and fill the hollow with a few of the crushed pistachios, and seal it
by squeezing the mixture over it and then rolling the ball once more.

Heat a thin layer of oil in a heavy-bottomed frying pan/skillet.
Place the meatballs in the pan and cook them on all sides, until nicely
browned. Drain on kitchen paper/paper towels, sprinkle with the
remaining crushed pistachios, and serve with lemon wedges to squeeze
over them.

AN AFRICAN CLASSIC, THIS TASTY ONE-POT OF RICE, TOMATOES AND CHICKEN IS AN EXAMPLE OF HEARTY COMFORT FOOD THAT CAN NOW BE FOUND ACROSS THE WORLD STREET-FOOD SCENE.

JOLLOF RICE

450 g/1 lb. tomatoes
2 tablespoons vegetable oil
4 chicken breast fillets, chopped
1 onion, peeled and chopped
1 garlic clove, peeled and chopped
½ red (bell) pepper, chopped
300 g/heaping 1½ cups long-grain rice, rinsed
1 carrot, peeled and sliced
50 g/1 cup green beans, topped, tailed and sliced
2 tablespoons tomato purée/paste
1 Scotch bonnet or habanero chilli/chile, finely chopped
350 ml/1⅓ cup chicken or vegetable stock
a pinch of salt
chopped fresh flat-leaf parsley, to garnish

SERVES 6

Begin by scalding the tomatoes. Pour boiling water over them in a heatproof bowl. Set aside for 1 minute, then drain and gently peel off the skin using a sharp knife. Roughly chop, reserving any juices, and set aside.

Heat 1 tablespoon of the oil in a heavy-bottomed casserole dish set over a medium heat. Add the chicken and fry, stirring, for a few minutes until lightly browned; season with salt and remove with a slotted spoon.

Put the remaining oil in the casserole dish. Add the onion, garlic and (bell) pepper and fry, stirring, for 2–3 minutes, until softened. Add the chopped tomatoes with their juices, cover, bring to a boil and cook for 5 minutes, stirring now and then.

Add the fried chicken, rice, carrot and green beans and mix in the tomato purée/paste. Add the Scotch bonnet or habanero chilli/ chile, pour in the stock and season with salt. Bring to a boil, cover, reduce the heat and cook for 25–30 minutes until the liquid has been absorbed and the rice is tender. Garnish with parsley and serve at once.

WHAT CAN BE EASIER THAN A SNACK YOU CAN CARRY ON A STICK? LIKE MANY OF THE DISHES IN THIS BOOK, THESE KEBABS/KABOBS ARE THE TYPE OF STREET FOOD THAT HAS MANY VARIATIONS AND CAN BE FOUND IN COUNTRIES ALL AROUND THE WORLD. MARINATING CHICKEN IS SUCH A SIMPLE BUT EFFECTIVE WAY OF ADDING FLAVOUR. SERVE WITH BASMATI RICE, A TZATZIKI DIP OR A RAITA AND A SIDE SALAD.

SAFFRON GARLIC CHICKEN KEBABS

a generous pinch
   of saffron threads
2 garlic cloves
3 tablespoons olive oil,
   plus extra for
   basting
freshly squeezed juice
   of ½ lemon
500 g/1 lb. 2 oz.
   chicken breast fillet,
   cut into about
   2.5-cm/1-inch cubes

a pinch of salt
torn fresh mint leaves,
   to garnish

8 wooden skewers,
   soaked in water

SERVES 4

Grind the saffron threads, then soak in 1 teaspoon of warm water.

Pound the garlic into a paste and mix with a pinch of salt.

Mix together the garlic, saffron water, olive oil, lemon juice and salt in a large bowl to make the marinade. Add the chicken and toss, coating thoroughly in the marinade. Cover and marinate in the fridge for 4–6 hours, turning over the chicken pieces halfway through.

Preheat the grill/broiler until very hot. Thread the marinated chicken onto the skewers, dividing the pieces evenly.

Grill the chicken kebabs/kabobs for about 15 minutes until cooked through and the juices run clear, turning often and basting with a little oil if required. Serve at once, garnished with fresh mint.

CHICKPEAS OFTEN FEATURE IN THE TAGINES OF ARID MOROCCAN AREAS AS THEY PROVIDE NOURISHMENT WHERE OTHER FOODS ARE SCARCE. COMBINED WITH VEGETABLES AND SPICES, THEY MAKE FOR A HEARTY TAGINE, ALSO POPULAR IN THE STALLS OF FES AND MARRAKESH.

SPICY CARROT & CHICKPEA TAGINE

2 tablespoons ghee
  or 1 tablespoon olive oil
  plus 1 tablespoon butter
1 large onion, finely
  chopped
1–2 red chillies/chiles,
  seeded and finely
  chopped
2–3 garlic cloves, finely
  chopped
2 teaspoons cumin seeds
2 teaspoons coriander
  seeds
1–2 teaspoons sugar
2–3 carrots, peeled, halved
  lengthways and thickly
  sliced

2 x 400-g/14-oz.
  cans of chickpeas,
  drained and rinsed
2 teaspoons ground
  turmeric
1 teaspoon ground
  cinnamon
a bunch of fresh
  coriander/cilantro,
  leaves finely chopped
sea salt and freshly
  ground black pepper

SERVES 4

Heat the ghee in the base of a tagine or in a heavy-bottomed saucepan, stir in the onion, chillies/chiles, garlic, cumin and coriander seeds and the sugar and fry for 2–3 minutes, until the onion begins to colour. Toss in the carrots and cook for an additional 1–2 minutes, then add the chickpeas.

Stir in the turmeric and cinnamon and pour in enough water to cover the base of the tagine. Bring the water to a boil, put on the lid, and cook over a gentle heat for 20–25 minutes, topping up the water if necessary, until the carrots are tender.

Season the tagine with salt and pepper, stir in most of the coriander/cilantro, and garnish with the remainder.

BAKLAVA IS THE TIP OF THE SWEET ICEBERG IN TURKEY. LAYERS OF DELICATE YET CRISP FILO/PHYLLO PASTRY LADEN WITH HONEY, SPICES AND NUTS - TRADITIONALLY PISTACHIOS - ARE HARD TO RESIST IN THEIR BITE-SIZED SHAPES. THIS RECIPE USES MAPLE SYRUP AND COCONUT OIL, WHICH WORK WONDERFULLY WITH THE SPICED NUTTY FILLING.

BAKLAVA

200 g/1⅓ cups shelled unsalted pistachios, plus 1 tablespoon extra to serve
100 g/²/₃ cup whole almonds
100 g/²/₃ cup whole pecan nuts
150 g/³/₄ cup coconut palm sugar
good pinch of sea salt
½ teaspoon ground cinnamon
¼ teaspoon ground cardamom
5 tablespoons coconut oil or butter, melted
20 filo/phyllo sheets, cut into 15 x 25-cm/6 x 12-inch rectangles

SYRUP
180 ml/³/₄ cup pure maple syrup
120 ml/½ cup water
1 cinnamon stick
freshly squeezed juice of ½ an orange
freshly squeezed juice and zest of ½ a lemon
2 cardamom pods, bashed open

a 15 x 25-cm/6 x 10-inch cake pan, lined with parchment paper

SERVES 12

For the syrup, place all the ingredients in a saucepan and bring to a boil. Reduce the heat to low and simmer for 5 minutes until slightly reduced. Remove from the heat and let cool. Strain through a sieve/strainer and refrigerate.

Preheat the oven to 180°C (360°F) Gas 4.

Place half the nuts and the coconut palm sugar, salt, ground cinnamon and cardamom in a food processor. Blitz until very finely chopped. Add in the remaining nuts and blitz until finely chopped, but not quite as finely as the first half, so they have a bit of a bite.

Using a pastry brush, brush the parchment paper in your lined cake pan with a little of the melted coconut butter or oil. Place one filo/phyllo sheet into the pan and generously brush with oil, but do not let it pool, repeat 5 times so you have 6 oiled sheets. Place half the nut mixture on top and spread out. Layer another 6 filo/phyllo sheets on top, oiling each sheet generously.

Spread the rest of the nut mixture on top and finish with the last 8 sheets of filo/phyllo, brushing with oil as before. Press firmly down on the baklava so it is well compacted.

Using a very sharp knife, cut the baklava into bite-sized rectangle or diamond shapes; take your time so as not to tear the pastry. Bake for 45–50 minutes until the pastry is golden brown on top. If it is beginning to burn, cover with foil. The filo/phyllo pastry will curl up once baked. To avoid this, you can sprinkle water onto the baklava prior to baking, if you prefer it this way.

Remove the baklava from the oven and immediately pour the cold syrup over it, ensuring it seeps into every crevice. Let cool completely before serving. Do not cover or refrigerate as the filo/phyllo will become soggy. When ready to serve, chop the remaining 1 tablespoon of pistachio nuts and sprinkle over the top.

AN ASIAN ADVENTURE

DIFFERENT VERSIONS OF THE SPRING ROLL CAN BE FOUND IN MANY ASIAN COUNTRIES. THIS VIETNAMESE VERSION IS TRADITIONALLY EATEN HOT WITH HERBS WRAPPED AROUND THEM AND DIPPED INTO A SWEET-SPICY SAUCE.

SPRING ROLLS

24 fresh square spring roll pastry wrappers, about 14 cm/5½ inches, thawed if frozen
up to 3 litres/3 quarts sunflower or vegetable oil, for deep frying

FILLING
3 tablespoons dried shredded wood ear mushrooms
50 g/1¾ oz. glass (cellophane) noodles
250 g/9 oz. minced/ ground chicken or pork
175 g/6 oz. king prawns/jumbo shrimp, shelled, deveined and coarsely chopped
120 g/4 oz. canned (lump) crabmeat, squeezed of excess moisture
250 g/9 oz. white yam, peeled and julienned
2 carrots, shredded
120 g/2 cups beansprouts
1 tablespoon sugar

1 pork stock cube
a pinch of coarse black pepper
a pinch of sea salt
2 spring onions/ scallions, thinly sliced
2 garlic cloves, finely chopped

DIPPING SAUCE
2 garlic cloves, finely chopped
2 Bird's Eye chillies/ chiles, finely chopped
2 tablespoons cider vinegar
2 tablespoons fish sauce
2 tablespoons sugar

TO SERVE (OPTIONAL)
lettuce leaves
Thai sweet basil
coriander/cilantro
hot mint

a deep-fat fryer (optional)

MAKES 24

For the filling, put the wood ear mushrooms in a bowl, cover with warm water and let soak for at least 30 minutes. When ready, drain the mushrooms and pat them dry.

Cook the noodles according to the instructions given on the package. Drain, pat dry and cut into short lengths.

When you are ready to assemble the rolls, make sure all the filling ingredients are prepared, dry and mixed together. Start to heat up your deep fat fryer, or a large, deep pan half-filled with oil over medium heat. Heat the oil to 140°C/285°F, until a cube of bread dropped in sizzles and browns in 1 minute.

Place a pastry wrapper diagonally in front of you. Spoon 1 tablespoon of the filling towards the lower corner. Fold the 2 side corners inward over the filling, as if making an envelope, then fold the bottom corner over. Roll up the package tightly, tucking in the filling in a neat cylinder as you roll it towards the far corner. Seal the flap with a touch of oil. Deep-fry the roll for 4–5 minutes until golden. Remove and drain on kitchen paper/paper towel, taste, then adjust the seasoning of the remaining filling if needed. Now assemble and deep fry the remaining rolls in batches.

For the dipping sauce, mix together the garlic, chillies/chiles and vinegar in a bowl. Set aside for 2 minutes. This 'cooks' the garlic. Now add the fish sauce, sugar and 400 ml/1½ cups water.

If you like, wrap each roll in a lettuce leaf with the herbs and serve with the dipping sauce in small individual bowls.

AS QUICK AS YOU LIKE, TEMPURA BARS IN JAPAN WILL MAKE YOU PRETTY
MUCH ANYTHING BATTERED, FRIED AND SERVED UP IN SECONDS! HERE YOU GET
ASSORTED VEGETABLES, WITH A LITTLE HEAT FROM A WASABI MAYONNAISE DIP.

VEGETABLE TEMPURA

WASABI MAYONNAISE (optional)
300 ml/1¼ cups good extra
   virgin olive oil
300 ml/1¼ cups sunflower oil
2 egg yolks
1 teaspoon Dijon mustard
squeeze of lemon juice
a pinch of salt
3 teaspoons wasabi powder
   or paste

selection of vegetables,
   e.g. carrot, sweet potato,
   aubergine/eggplant, squash,
   broccoli, (bell) pepper, spring
   onion/scallion, courgette/
   zucchini, asparagus,
   mushrooms
600 ml/2½ cups vegetable,
   sunflower or rapeseed oil
100 g/¾ cup rice flour, plus
   extra for coating
100 g/¾ cup cornflour/
   cornstarch
1 teaspoon baking powder
small bottle of ice-cold
   sparkling water
2 egg whites
few cubes of ice
sea salt and freshly ground
   black pepper
Wasabi Mayonnaise (see above),
   to serve

MAKES 8

First make the Wasabi Mayonnaise. Combine the oils in a jug/pitcher.
Put the egg yolks, Dijon mustard, lemon juice and a pinch of salt in the
food processor bowl or a mixing bowl. As you start to process/beat with
an electric hand mixer, very slowly feed in the oils a little at a time until
the mixture begins to emulsify and come together.

Once this happens you can add the oil a bit faster, but never be
tempted to put it all in at once as the mayonnaise will split. Have a little
cup of hot water ready, as a few drops added in when it is looking like it
might split usually brings it back together. Once you have added all the
oil, stir in the wasabi powder or paste and refrigerate until needed.

Cut the hard vegetables into thin slices about ½ cm/¼ inch thick.
Cut softer vegetables like aubergine/eggplant, spring onion/scallion
or (bell) pepper a little thicker.

If you have a deep fat fryer, heat the oil to 190°C/375°F; if not then
heat it in a deep saucepan. Check the temperature by dropping a
breadcrumb into the oil. It should turn golden in about 25–30 seconds.
Any faster than this and the tempura will burn before the vegetable
inside is cooked through.

While the oil is heating, mix together the flours, baking powder,
½ teaspoon salt and a good pinch of pepper in a bowl. Slowly stir in just
enough cold sparkling water until you have a yogurt consistency, but
don't over-beat. It doesn't matter if the batter is lumpy; traditionally
Japanese tempura batter is not mixed too thoroughly, as the lumps in
the batter help to form a more crunchy tempura. Using an electric hand
mixer, beat the egg whites in a separate bowl until they form hard
peaks. Fold the eggs into the batter, stir the ice cubes through to keep
it as cold as possible.

Lightly coat the vegetables in rice flour. Shake off any excess,
then dip into the batter. Carefully place them into the hot oil. Don't
overcrowd the fryer or pan, as it will bring down the temperature of the
oil. The vegetables should cook in about 2 minutes. Remove all the
tempura with a slotted spoon and drain on kitchen paper/paper towels.
Serve with the Wasabi Mayonnaise.

ALTHOUGH SUSHI IS OFTEN MISTAKEN AS A REFERENCE TO THE FISH FOUND IN SOME SUSHI RECIPES, IT IS ACTUALLY THE VINEGARED RICE IN THIS VERSATILE JAPANESE DISH THAT'S MADE ITS WAY FROM THE STREET-FOOD COUNTER TO GOURMET RESTAURANTS AROUND THE WORLD. IN THIS RECIPE, BULGUR WHEAT MAKES AN INTERESTING ALTERNATIVE, BUT YOU COULD USE EITHER BROWN OR WHITE RICE, IF PREFERRED, FOR A MORE TRADITIONAL DISH. EITHER WAY, THIS VEGGIE SUSHI IS A TREAT THAT'S NOT AS HARD TO MAKE AS IT LOOKS.

SUSHI

200 g/1¼ cups bulgur wheat
a pinch of salt
1 tablespoon seasoned rice
    vinegar
1 small carrot, peeled
½ small cucumber, peeled
1 small avocado
4 sheets nori seaweed
4 tablespoons store-bought
    almond and parsley pesto
    (or other green pesto)
Japanese Dipping Sauce,
    to serve (see page 107)

a sushi mat

SERVES 4

First prepare the Japanese Dipping Sauce and set aside until ready to serve.

Place the bulgur wheat in a saucepan with 500 ml/ 2 cups water and a pinch of salt. Heat gently until boiling. Cover with a tight-fitting lid and cook over a very low heat for 20 minutes. Remove from the heat, drain any excess water and leave to go cold.

Transfer the cold bulgur wheat to a bowl and stir in the seasoned vinegar.

Cut the carrot and cucumber into equal-sized 5-cm/ 2-inch batons. Peel, stone/pit and thinly slice the avocado.

Place a sushi mat on a flat surface with the slats going from left to right and top with a nori seaweed sheet. Take a quarter of the bulgur wheat and very carefully spread over the nori, leaving a 2-cm/¾-inch border at the side furthest from you. Build the bulgur wheat up slightly to form a mound in front of the clear border. Lay a quarter of the carrots, cucumber and avocado along the side nearest to you. Carefully spread the pesto along the top of the vegetables.

Very carefully pull the mat up and forward, rolling the seaweed and filling up tightly into a log, pressing firmly as you go all the way to the far side. Roll the mat completely around the sushi briefly to help seal. Remove the mat, wrap in clingfilm/plastic wrap and refrigerate until required.

Repeat with the remaining sushi to make 4 rolls in total. To serve, unwrap from the clingfilm/plastic wrap and, using a sharp knife, cut into 6 thick pieces and serve with the Japanese Dipping Sauce.

DIM SUM IS A STYLE OF ONE-BITE CHINESE CUISINE SERVED IN THE STEAMER BASKETS YOU CAN SEE STACKED HIGH AT STREET FOOD STALLS, OR WHEN BROUGHT TO YOU AT A RESTAURANT TABLE. ALSO KNOWN AS *HAR GAO*, THIS LITTLE DUMPLING IS ONE OF THE MOST ICONIC DIM SUM DISHES. THE CRYSTAL SKIN SHOULD BE DELICATE ENOUGH TO JUST ABOUT SEE THE PINK PRAWNS/SHRIMP PEEPING THROUGH.

TRADITIONAL PRAWN DUMPLINGS

CRYSTAL SKIN DOUGH
100 g/³/₄ cup wheat starch
50 g/½ cup tapioca flour/starch
a pinch of fine salt
150 ml/²/₃ cup boiling (not just hot) water

FILLING
50 g/1³/₄ oz. firm tofu, drained and sliced
150 g/5¼ oz. raw prawns/shrimp, peeled, deveined and chopped into small pieces
1 teaspoon fresh ginger, peeled and grated
1 teaspoon crushed garlic
½ teaspoon Shaoxing rice wine
½ teaspoon salt
½ teaspoon sugar
½ teaspoon ground white pepper
1 teaspoon olive oil
1 teaspoon cornflour/cornstarch

DIPPING SAUCE
1 small piece fresh ginger, peeled and grated
6 tablespoons black vinegar

a bamboo steamer, lined with parchment paper

MAKES 16

Squeeze out the excess water from the tofu and finely mince using a sharp knife.

Place the prawns/shrimp in a bowl. Add the tofu, ginger, garlic, Shaoxing rice wine, salt, sugar, white pepper, oil, and cornflour/cornstarch. Mix well and set aside in the fridge to marinate while you make the dough.

In a large mixing bowl, combine all the ingredients and mix into a dough. Transfer to a lightly floured surface and knead until smooth. Separate the dough in half and roll into two equal logs. Wrap in clingfilm/plastic wrap. Let rest. Divide the dough into 16 equal balls. On a lightly floured surface use a rolling pin to flatten the balls into discs, 5 cm/2 inches in diameter. Cover the finished skins with a damp tea/kitchen towel as you work so that they don't dry out.

Place a large teaspoon of filling neatly into the centre of a skin. Fold the skin in half over the filling. Pinch one end together and start to crimp the edge by making small folds to form pleats to create the traditional crescent shape.

Put the dumplings into the bamboo steamer and steam over boiling water for 15–20 minutes, until the skin is transparent and the prawns/shrimp are red.

To make the Dipping Sauce, stir the ginger into the black vinegar and serve alongside the hot dumplings.

THERE ARE MANY TYPES OF BAO IN ASIA, BUT THESE SMOOTH, PILLOWY AND FASHIONABLE CLAMSHELL-SHAPED BUNS REALLY SHOW OFF THE VIBRANT COLOURS OF VEGETABLES – AND ARE THE PERFECT SIZE TO HOLD IN YOUR FINGERTIPS!

VEGETABLE CLAMSHELL BAO BUNS

DOUGH

2 teaspoons easy-bake dry yeast

450 g/3½ cups Asian white wheat flour

100 g/¾ cup plus 1 tablespoon icing sugar/confectioners' sugar, sifted

15 g/2 tablespoons dried milk powder

¼ teaspoon fine salt

2 teaspoons baking powder

180 ml/¾ cup water, add more if needed

50 ml/scant ¼ cup vegetable oil, plus extra for oiling the bowl

VEGETABLE FILLING

1 head of Chinese cabbage leaves

3 handfuls Chinese spinach

2 small leeks

2 tablespoons sunflower oil, plus extra for oiling the dough

1 carrot, peeled and grated

8 oyster mushrooms, sliced

3 Chinese chive stems, white parts removed, sliced

a large handful of fresh coriander/cilantro, finely chopped

vegetarian stir-fry sauce, to serve

a bamboo steamer, lined with parchment paper

Makes 16

Place the yeast in a large mixing bowl, then add the flour, sugar, milk powder, salt and baking powder. Make sure the yeast is separated from the salt by the layer of flour. Add the water and oil and bring together with a dough scraper. When no dry flour remains, place the dough on a lightly floured surface. Knead firmly for 5–10 minutes, until smooth and elastic.

Lightly oil the mixing bowl. Shape the dough into two cylinders and place back in the oiled bowl, cover with oiled clingfilm/plastic wrap and leave in a warm place to rise for 40–60 minutes, until doubled in size.

Remove the risen dough from the bowl, punch it down and knead it again briefly, but very carefully rather than firmly this time. Roll the dough out into a big rectangle and portion it out into 16 equal balls. Cover the dough balls with oiled clingfilm/plastic wrap and let rest again for 30 minutes in a warm place.

Roll out each dough ball so that it has a diameter of around 7.5 cm/3 inches and flatten each slightly with a rolling pin into an oval shape, around 12 x 6 cm/4½ x 2⅓ inches.

Cut parchment paper into 16 squares, each 12 cm/4 ½ inches square. Use your fingers to lightly oil the surface of a piece of dough, place a square of paper on top and fold the dough in half so that the paper is in the centre. Cut another 16 squares of parchment paper just larger than the buns. Lay the paper squares on a baking sheet and lightly dust with flour. Place a bun on top of each square on its side, cover with oiled clingfilm/plastic wrap and leave to rise for 30–40 minutes.

While the buns are rising, slice the cabbage leaves, spinach and leeks lengthwise into ribbons about 6 cm/2¼ inches long and 2 cm/¾ inch thick. Set aside.

Brush the top of each risen bun with sunflower oil. Lift the buns on their squares and place in the bamboo steamer about 4 cm/1½ inches apart. Steam over boiling water for 15–20 minutes until light and fluffy.

Heat the sunflower oil in a wok and stir-fry all the vegetables and herbs for around 2–3 minutes. Add the stir-fry sauce to taste and quickly toss the vegetables.

When the buns are ready, remove the parchment paper and fill with the hot vegetables to serve.

GYOZA IS A JAPANESE RECIPE THAT IS SIMILAR TO CHINESE DUMPLINGS, BUT IS KNOWN TO BE A MORE MODERN CREATION. EQUALLY VERSATILE, YOU CAN MAKE GYOZA WITH ALL TYPES OF FILLING, FOR ALL TYPES OF TASTE!

SALMON & SPRING ONION GYOZA

DASHI BROTH
15 g/1 tablespoon chopped dried kombu
15 g/1 tablespoon dried bonito flakes

JAPANESE DIPPING SAUCE
200 ml/³/₄ cup Dashi Broth (see above)
3 tablespoons Japanese soy sauce
3 tablespoons mirin
½ teaspoon caster/granulated sugar

250 g/9 oz. skinless salmon fillet, boned
2 spring onions/scallions, trimmed and thinly sliced
1 tablespoon mirin
1 tablespoon light soy sauce
20 gyoza wrappers
1 tablespoon grapeseed oil
½ quantity Japanese Dipping Sauce (see above)
black sesame seeds and micro herbs, to serve

a baking sheet, lined with baking parchment

SERVES 4

Begin by preparing the Dashi broth. Pour 1.25 litres/2 pints cold water into a saucepan, add the kombu and set aside for 30 minutes to soften. Bring the mixture to the boil over a medium heat, removing any scum that appears on the surface, then reduce the heat and simmer gently for 10 minutes.

Remove the pan from the heat, stir in the bonito flakes and allow the broth to cool. Strain with a fine mesh sieve/strainer and use immediately or chill until required. The broth will keep stored in an airtight container for 3 days in the fridge or can be frozen for up to 1 month.

Now prepare the Japanese Dipping Sauce. Beat all the ingredients together in a bowl or, put all the ingredients into a jar, screw on the lid and shake well. Set aside or store in a sterilized glass jar with an airtight lid in the fridge until it is all used up.

Next prepare the salmon. Cut the fillet into small cubes and put in a large mixing bowl. Add the spring onions/scallions, mirin and soy sauce, and stir well to combine.

Working one at a time, lay the gyoza wrappers out flat and place a teaspoon of the mixture on one half of each wrapper. Dampen the edges with a little cold water, fold the wrapper over the filling and carefully press the edges together to seal.

Preheat the oven to 110°C (225°F) Gas ¼ (or the lowest heat setting).

Heat the oil in a wok or large non-stick frying pan/skillet over a medium heat and fry half the gyoza on one side until really browned. Add 100 ml/¹/₃ cup water and simmer, partially covered, for 3 minutes until the water is evaporated. Fry for an additional minute until crisp. Transfer the gyoza to the prepared baking sheet, turn off the oven and set in the still-warm oven while you cook the remaining gyoza in the same way.

- 400 g/2 cups dried moong dal (skinned and split mung beans), soaked overnight
- 2 tablespoons soy sauce, plus extra to serve
- 4 garlic cloves, crushed
- 1 tablespoon fresh ginger, peeled and grated
- 4 tablespoons vegetable oil
- 250 g/8 oz. minced/ground lean pork
- 1 teaspoon salt
- 1 leek, trimmed and finely chopped
- 125 g/4 oz. green beans, fresh or frozen, chopped into small pieces
- sliced red chilli/chile and chopped pickled cucumber to serve

MAKES ABOUT 12

THESE SAVOURY PANCAKES OFTEN CONTAIN KIMCHI, THE KOREAN SPICED PICKLED CABBAGE THAT IS BECOMING INCREASINGLY POPULAR IN MUCH FUSION COOKING ALL AROUND THE WORLD. THESE PANCAKES USE GREEN BEANS INSTEAD, FOR A LIGHTER TASTE. EITHER WAY, THEY MAKE A DELICIOUS SAVOURY SNACK, BEST SERVED AS THEY WOULD BE AT A KOREAN FOOD MARKET - IMMEDIATELY AFTER FRYING.

MOONG PANCAKES WITH PORK

Drain the moong dal and put them in the food processor. Blend them finely, then add 400 ml/1²/₃ cups of water, the soy sauce, all but 1 crushed garlic clove and all but 1 teaspoon of the grated ginger. Process the mixture to a smooth purée.

Heat 2 tablespoons of the oil in a frying pan/skillet or wok and fry the remaining garlic for 1 minute before adding the pork, together with the remaining teaspoon of grated ginger and the salt. Stir well and continue to cook until the pork is cooked through, then add the chopped leek and green beans and continue to cook gently until the vegetables are half-cooked, but not soft. Take off the heat and set aside. Transfer the moong dal purée to a bowl, then leave the batter to sit for at least 30 minutes.

Heat a teaspoon of the oil in a non-stick frying pan/skillet over a medium heat, and when it is hot, pour a spoonful of the batter into the pan/skillet. Spread out the batter with the back of the ladle until it forms a 8-cm/3-inch circle. Repeat the process with more batter, frying several pancakes at a time.

Cook the pancakes until golden brown on the underside and until tiny holes have begun to appear on the upper surface, then flip them over and cook the other side. This will probably take around 5 minutes on each side. It is important not to overheat the pan and burn the surface before the inside is cooked, but it must be hot enough for the pancakes to brown and crisp.

Keep warm while you make the other pancakes in the same way, brushing the frying pan/skillet or wok with oil before cooking each batch. Serve straight away with a bowl of soy sauce for dipping, and pickled cucumber and some sliced red chilli/chile, if desired.

TEMPEH HAS BEEN EATEN AS AN EVERYDAY INDONESIAN SNACK FOR DECADES AND TODAY, IT IS USED AS A SOY-BASED MEAT ALTERNATIVE IN VEGAN COOKING. IT IS USUALLY FRIED TO SERVE IN CURRIES, SALADS OR SANDWICHES, BUT HERE IT'S SHAPED LIKE A PATTY AND FLAVOURED WELL TO BE EATEN SOLO, JUST HOW IT WOULD BE SOLD BY A STREET VENDOR.

TWICE-COOKED TEMPEH

1 small onion, finely chopped
2 garlic cloves, finely chopped
1 teaspoon ground coriander
1-cm/½-inch piece of root ginger, peeled and grated, or 1 teaspoon ginger paste
1 bay leaf
1-cm/½-inch piece of fresh galangal, peeled and chopped, or teaspoon ground galangal
1 generous teaspoon soft brown sugar (optional)
½ teaspoon chilli/chili powder
1 teaspoon tamarind concentrate, dissolved in 250 ml/1 cup warm water
350 g/12 oz. tempeh, cut into 1 cm/½ inch thick bite-sized slices
1–2 tablespoons groundnut/peanut or vegetable oil

SERVES 3–4

Put all the ingredients, except the tempeh and the oil, into a medium pan and bring to a boil, then reduce the heat to a simmer.

Add the tempeh to the pan. Add water to cover and cook gently for 40 minutes, until all the liquid has been absorbed by the tempeh. Keep a close eye as the liquid is absorbed so that the tempeh doesn't burn. Set aside and let cool.

Heat the oil in a heavy-bottomed frying pan/skillet. Add the slices of tempeh and fry until golden and starting to crisp, about 3–4 minutes on each side. Drain on kitchen paper/paper towels and cool. Serve warm or cold.

These can be stored in an air-tight container in the fridge for up to a week.

ANOTHER ONE OF THE MOST VERSATILE FOODS IN CHINESE CUISINE, WONTONS ARE A TYPE OF DUMPLING THAT CAN BE FILLED WITH AN ENDLESS LIST OF SAVOURY FILLINGS. DEEP-FRYING THESE DUMPLINGS UNTIL THEY ARE CRISP TRANSFORMS THEM TO HAVE AN APPETIZING CRUNCH; WHEN SERVED WITH THE DIPPING SAUCE, THEY GO PERFECTLY WITH PRE-DINNER DRINKS. CHINESE BLACK RICE VINEGAR IS AVAILABLE FROM ASIAN STORES.

CRISPY GARLIC CHIVE CHICKEN WONTONS

1 chicken breast fillet (about 140 g/ 5 oz.), finely diced
4 tablespoons finely chopped fresh Chinese chives
a pinch of ground Sichuan pepper
1 teaspoon light soy sauce
½ teaspoon sesame oil
16 wonton wrappers
sunflower or vegetable oil, for deep frying

salt and freshly ground black pepper

DIPPING SAUCE
2 tablespoons Chinese black rice vinegar
1 teaspoon sugar
1 garlic clove, finely chopped
1 red chilli/chile, finely chopped (optional)

SERVES 4

Thoroughly mix together the diced chicken, Chinese chives, Sichuan pepper, soy sauce and sesame oil. Season well with salt and pepper.

Mix together the ingredients for the dipping sauce and set aside.

Take a wonton wrapper and place a teaspoon of the chicken mixture in the centre of the wrapper. Brush the edges with a little cold water and bring the wrapper together over the chicken to form a parcel, pressing together well to seal properly. Set aside. Repeat the process until all 16 wrappers have been filled.

Heat the oil in a large saucepan until very hot. Add four of the wontons and fry for a few minutes, until golden brown on both sides, turning over halfway through to ensure even browning. Remove with a slotted spoon and drain on kitchen paper. Repeat the process with the remaining wontons.

Serve at once with the dipping sauce.

NOT TO BE CONFUSED WITH MEDITERRANEAN CALAMARI, SALT AND PEPPER SQUID CAN BE FOUND ACROSS THE ASIAN CONTINENT, IN CANTONESE KITCHENS OR ALONG THE VIETNAMESE COASTLINE, WHERE IT CAN BE FOUND AS A SNACK AT A BAR, A STREET FOOD BITE OR AS AN APPETIZER AT SOMEWHERE A LITTLE MORE FANCY.

SALT & PEPPER SQUID

½ teaspoon ground Sansho pepper
2 teaspoons sea salt
65 g/½ cup rice flour
450 g/1 lb. squid, cleaned and sliced
freshly squeezed juice of 1 lemon
vegetable oil, for frying

SANSHO SPICY DIP
115 g/½ cup good-quality mayonnaise
5 g/¼ cup Vietnamese or regular basil leaves
½ teaspoon Sansho pepper
½ teaspoon sea salt
grated zest of 1 lemon

SERVES 4

To make the dip, beat all the ingredients together in a small bowl until well combined. Set aside.

In a large shallow bowl mix together the Sansho pepper, salt and rice flour. Put the squid in another bowl and pour over the lemon juice.

Pour enough oil to come halfway up a large saucepan, then place over a medium–high heat until the oil starts to simmer.

Take a few pieces of squid at a time and toss in the flour mixture to coat. Working in batches, deep fry for 2–3 minutes until golden and cooked through. Transfer to a wire rack to drain.

Pile the cooked squid in a shallow bowl and serve with Sansho Spicy Dip.

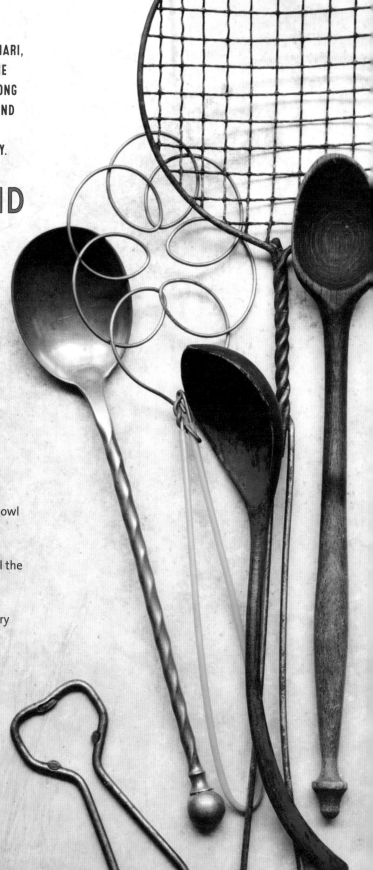

YAKITORI LITERALLY MEANS GRILLED CHICKEN BUT OFTEN REFERS TO ANY SKEWERED FOODS COOKED WITH A GLAZE. SERVED AT FOOD COURTS, SPORTS MATCHES AND FROM OTHER STREET FOOD VENDORS ACROSS JAPAN, THESE SALT-SWEET SKEWERS ARE A GREAT CROWD PLEASER! SERVE SIMPLY WITH JASMINE OR SUSHI RICE AND BLANCHED PAK CHOI/BOK CHOY OR SPINACH.

YAKITORI-GLAZED MUSHROOM & CHICKEN SKEWERS

16 white/cup mushrooms, stems trimmed off
250 g/9 oz. boneless chicken breast, cut into short, thin strips
16 fresh shiitake mushrooms, halved, stems trimmed off
1 green (bell) pepper, seeded and cut into 2- x 2-cm/^{3}/$_4$- x ^{3}/$_4$-inch squares
2 spring onions/scallions, cut into 2-cm/^{3}/$_4$-inch lengths
sliced red chilli/chile, to garnish (optional)

YAKITORI GLAZE
50 ml/3 tablespoons rice wine or Amontillado sherry
50 ml/3 tablespoons mirin
50 ml/3 tablespoons light soy sauce
1 tablespoon white granulated sugar
^{1}/$_4$ teaspoon salt

8 metal skewers or wooden skewers soaked in water

SERVES 4

Make the yakitori glaze by placing the rice wine or sherry, mirin, soy sauce, sugar and salt in a small saucepan. Bring to a boil and boil for 1 minute until melted together into a syrupy glaze. Turn off the heat.

Thread the white/cup mushrooms, chicken, shiitake mushrooms, green (bell) pepper and spring onions/scallions onto the 8 skewers.

Preheat a grill/broiler to medium–high heat. Brush the skewers generously with the yakitori glaze and then grill the skewers for 8–10 minutes until the chicken is cooked through, brushing repeatedly with the glaze and turning over the skewers halfway through. Serve at once garnished with the red chilli/chile, if liked.

NOODLE SOUPS ARE A POPULAR DISH IN ASIAN CUISINE AND A MALAYSIAN LAKSA IS ONE OF THE SPICIER ONES! MADE WITH COCONUT MILK AND SEAFOOD, PORK OR CHICKEN, IT IS ALWAYS SERVED WITH A SELECTION OF GARNISHES. DRAWING ON A RICH CULTURAL HERITAGE, THE USE OF SPICES AND COCONUT CREATES A TRULY UNIQUE SOUP.

CHICKEN LAKSA

250 g/9 oz. dried rice
  stick noodles
2 large skinless
  chicken breast fillets
  (about 350 g/12 oz.)
1 litre/1³/₄ pints
  chicken stock
2 tablespoons
  vegetable oil
400 ml/1²/₃ cups
  coconut milk
200 ml/³/₄ cup coconut
  cream
2 tablespoons fish
  sauce
2 teaspoons caster/
  granulated sugar

LAKSA PASTE
6 shallots, chopped
4 garlic cloves,
  chopped
2 lemongrass stems,
  thinly sliced
2 large red Bird's Eye
  chillies/chiles,
  seeded and sliced
2.5 cm/1 inch fresh
  galangal, peeled
  and chopped

2.5 cm/1 inch fresh
  turmeric, peeled
  and chopped (or
  1 teaspoon ground
  turmeric)
4 macadamia nuts
1 tablespoon shrimp
  paste
2 teaspoons coriander
  seeds, toasted and
  ground

TO SERVE
beansprouts, trimmed
½ cucumber, sliced
deep-fried puffed tofu
  (optional)
deep-fried shallots
  (optional)
fresh coriander/
  cilantro or
  Vietnamese mint
1 fresh lotus root,
  peeled and sliced
1 lime, cut into wedges
chilli/chili oil

SERVES 4

Soak the noodles in a bowlful of hot water for about 20–30 minutes until softened. Drain well, shake dry and set aside.

Put the chicken breasts in a saucepan with the stock set over a low–medium heat. Simmer very gently for 10 minutes until the chicken is just cooked. Remove the chicken from the stock and set aside to cool completely. Once cool, slice thinly.

To make the laksa paste, pound all the ingredients together using a large pestle and mortar or blitz in a food processor until smooth.

Heat the oil in a wok or non-stick saucepan set over a medium heat and add the laksa paste. Fry for 2 minutes until fragrant, then add the coconut milk and chicken stock. Simmer gently for 10 minutes and then stir in the coconut cream, fish sauce and sugar. Simmer gently for an additional 2–3 minutes.

Divide the noodles between bowls and add the sliced chicken. Pour over the hot soup and serve topped with a selection of the garnishes, as you like. Pass around some chilli/chili oil, to drizzle.

LIKE ALL JAPANESE DISHES, IT IS THE CONTRAST OF TEXTURES AND FLAVOURS THAT DEFINES THIS DISH. THE SOFT SLURP OF NOODLES IS BALANCED WITH THE CRISP TEMPURA BATTER WHICH, ONCE SUBMERGED INTO THE HOT STOCK, TURNS THIS INTO A COMFORTING ONE-BOWL DISH.

RAMEN WITH TEMPURA PRAWNS

8 large prawns/shrimp
1.5 litres/2½ pints Dashi Broth (see page 107)
125 ml/½ cup Japanese soy sauce
75 ml/scant ⅓ cup mirin
250 g/9 oz. dried ramen noodles
125 g/2 handfuls mangetout/snow peas, trimmed and thinly sliced
2 tablespoons dried wakame seaweed
150 g/1 cup plus 1 tablespoon cubed firm tofu
vegetable oil, for deep frying
2 large spring onions/scallions, trimmed and thinly sliced

TEMPURA BATTER
1 egg yolk
250 ml/1 cup iced water
100 g/¾ cup plain/all-purpose flour
2 tablespoons potato (or rice) flour

SERVES 4

Peel the prawns/shrimp, leaving the tail section intact and reserving the shells and head. Cut down the back of each one and pull out the black intestinal tract. Wash and dry the prawns/shrimp and set aside. Put the shells and heads in a saucepan set over a medium heat and pour in the Dashi Broth. Bring to a boil, cover and simmer for 30 minutes. Strain through a fine mesh sieve/strainer and return the stock to the pan. Add the soy sauce and mirin and set aside.

Plunge the noodles into a saucepan of boiling water and cook for about 4 minutes, until al dente. Drain, refresh under cold water and shake dry. Set aside.

To make the tempura batter, put the egg yolk, iced water and both flours in a large mixing bowl. Very lightly beat the mixture together using a fork to make a slightly lumpy but thin batter.

Return the broth mixture to a simmer, add the mange-tout/snow peas and seaweed and simmer for 2 minutes. Add the noodles and cook for 1 minute to heat through.

Meanwhile, heat about 5 cm/2 inches of oil in a wok until a cube of bread dropped into the oil crisps and turns brown in 20–30 seconds. Dip the prawns/shrimp into the tempura batter, shaking off any excess. Fry in batches for 2–3 minutes until crisp and golden. Carefully remove the cooked prawns/shrimp and drain on kitchen paper/paper towels. Add a little of the remaining tempura batter to the oil and cook until crisp. Drain this and put with the prawns/shrimp.

Divide the noodles between warmed soup bowls, add the tofu and spring onions/scallions, then pour over the soup. Top each with two tempura prawns/shrimp and sprinkle the crispy batter bits into the soup. Serve at once.

THIS DISH IS A STREET-FOOD FAVOURITE OF MANY VIETNAMESE PEOPLE WHEN THE SUN SETS - IT IS A LIGHT SAVOURY CRÊPE MADE WITH RICE FLOUR AND COCONUT MILK, TO BE EATEN ONCE IT'S COOKED. IT IS SERVED WITH AN ABUNDANCE OF SALAD LEAVES AND HERBS. EVERYTHING SHOULD BE PREPPED IN ADVANCE SO THE CRÊPES ARE READY AS SOON AS THEY ARE DONE.

SIZZLING CRÊPES WITH PORK AND PRAWNS

DIPPING SAUCE
2 garlic cloves, finely chopped
2 Bird's Eye chillies/chiles, finely chopped
2 tablespoons cider vinegar
5 tablespoons fish sauce
3 tablespoons sugar

CRÊPES
200 g/1½ cups rice flour
2 teaspoons ground turmeric
400 ml/1½ cups coconut milk
2 spring onions/scallions, thinly sliced
a pinch of sea salt
a pinch of sugar
vegetable or other cooking oil, for frying
4 shallots, chopped

200 g/7 oz. pork belly, thinly sliced
400 g/14 oz. king prawns/jumbo shrimp, shelled and deveined
200 g/3½ cups beansprouts
sea salt and black pepper

GARNISHES
lettuce leaves (optional)
spring onions/scallions, cut into short lengths
coriander/cilantro
Thai sweet basil
garden or hot mint

a 20-cm/8-inch non-stick frying pan/skillet with a lid

MAKES ABOUT 12

For the dipping sauce, mix together the garlic, chillies/chiles and vinegar in a bowl. Set aside for 2 minutes. This 'cooks' the garlic. Now add the fish sauce, sugar and 400 ml/1½ cups water.

To make the crêpes, mix together the flour, turmeric, coconut milk, 400 ml/1½ cups water, spring onions/scallions, salt and sugar in a bowl, making sure it is smooth and free of lumps.

Heat 1 teaspoon oil in the frying pan/skillet over medium heat and fry 1 teaspoon of the chopped shallots until browned. Season the pork belly and prawns/shrimp with salt and pepper and add a few pieces to the pan until cooked through. Set aside. Using a shallow ladle, pour in a thin layer of the crepe batter, and cover the pan with the lid. Let cook for 2 minutes. Remove the lid and cook for an additional minute, making sure the crepe is crispy and brown. Add the pork and prawns and a handful of beansprouts and fold the crêpe in half and set aside. Repeat this whole process with the remaining shallots, batter and other ingredients to make several more crepes.

To eat, break a piece of crêpe and add the spring onions/scallions and herbs, and dip it in the dipping sauce. You can roll it up in lettuce leaves, if you like.

BÁNH MÌ IS A VIETNAMESE BAGUETTE ORIGINALLY INSPIRED BY THE FRENCH. AS WITH MOST VIETNAMESE FOOD, THE LIGHTNESS OF THE FILLING INGREDIENTS IS VITAL – NO ONE RELISHES BEING WEIGHED DOWN. THE DOUGH IN THE CENTRE OF THE BAGUETTE IS REMOVED SO THAT YOU BITE STRAIGHT THROUGH THE LOVELY CRISP CRUST, DOWN TO THE FILLING WITHIN.

LEMONGRASS BEEF BAGUETTE

CHA CHIÊN VIETNAMESE HAM
500 g/1 lb. 2 oz. minced/ground pork (shoulder)
½ tablespoon (½ sachet) French baking powder (Alsa Levure Chimique "Alsacienne")
1 tablespoon sugar
2 tablespoons vegetable or other cooking oil, plus extra for oiling and frying
2 tablespoons fish sauce

LEMONGRASS BEEF
100 g/3½ oz. beef, thinly sliced
1 lemongrass stalk, finely chopped
1 garlic clove, finely chopped
1 shallot, finely chopped
1 teaspoon Maggi Seasoning (or soy sauce)
1 pork, chicken or vegetable stock cube
1 teaspoon sugar

PICKLE
2 carrots, shredded
½ daikon/mooli, shredded
5 tablespoons cider vinegar
5 tablespoons sugar

TO FILL
1 Vietnamese baguette or freshly baked, small French baguette
butter or soft cheese
pork or chicken liver pâté
Cha Chiên Vietnamese Ham, thinly sliced (see left)
coriander/cilantro
cucumber, cut into 10-cm/4-inch slivers
spring onions/ scallions, thinly sliced lengthways
Bird's Eye chillies/ chiles, thinly sliced
Maggi Seasoning (or soy sauce)
Sriracha chilli sauce

a steamer

SERVES 1

For the Vietnamese ham, put all the ingredients and 2 tablespoons water in a food processor and process until fine and well combined. Transfer the mixture to a bowl, cover and refrigerate for at least 4 hours or overnight.

Rub a little oil onto your hands. Shape the rested mixture into a large patty.

Grease the surface of the steamer and steam the ham for 5 minutes, until the juices run clear when you stick a knife in.

When ready to serve, heat a dash of oil in a frying pan/skillet and fry the patty, turning a couple of times, until golden brown all over. Set aside.

Next, for the lemongrass beef, preheat the oven to 220°C (425°F) Gas 7.

Mix all the ingredients in a bowl and marinate for 10 minutes. Transfer to a roasting pan and bake in the preheated oven for 15 minutes.

In the meantime, prepare the pickle. Mix all the ingredients in a bowl and let rest for 15 minutes. Drain and wring with your hands.

To fill and serve, slit the baguette lengthways and pull out the soft doughy inside (which can be used for breadcrumbs). Spread with butter or soft cheese and a smear of pâté. Layer the warm beef and its juices, pickle, cha chiên, coriander/cilantro, cucumber, spring onions/scallions and chillies/chiles over the top and squirt over a few drops of Maggi Seasoning and Srisacha chilli sauce.

All of Sài Gòn is perfumed with smoke from honey-grilled pork at lunchtime, bún tht nng (grilled/broiled meat on noodles) is a treat and a great example of Vietnamese cuisine: juicy, sweet and succulent meat with vermicelli, sharp pickles and herbs create layers of flavours and textures.

BBQ PORK-BELLY SKEWERS

1 lemongrass stalk, finely chopped

1 tablespoon galangal, finely chopped (optional)

2 shallots, finely chopped

4 garlic cloves, chopped

1 tablespoon honey

2 teaspoons fish sauce

2 tablespoons vegetable or other cooking oil

1 tablespoon tapioca flour/starch

½ teaspoon black pepper

1 tablespoon sugar

1 teaspoon shrimp paste

400 g/14 oz. pork belly, cut into bite-sized pieces

DIPPING SAUCE

4 tablespoons cider vinegar

4 tablespoons sugar

4 tablespoons fish sauce

2 garlic cloves, finely chopped

2 Bird's Eye chillies/chiles, finely chopped

NOODLE SALAD

300 g/10½ oz. thin rice vermicelli

a pinch of salt

a dash of vinegar

8 coriander/cilantro stems, torn

12 Thai sweet basil leaves, torn

12 cockscomb mint leaves (optional)

12 shiso/perilla leaves (optional)

8 lettuce leaves, torn

½ cucumber, julienned

Pickle (see page 126)

store-bought pickled leeks (optional)

4 tablespoons roasted salted peanuts, crushed

10–12 wooden skewers, soaked in water

SERVES 4

Put the lemongrass, galangal, shallots, garlic, honey, fish sauce, oil, tapioca flour/starch, pepper, sugar and shrimp paste in a bowl. Mix well and then rub the mixture into the pork pieces. Marinate in the fridge for 20 minutes.

Preheat the oven to 180°C (350°F) Gas 4, or preheat the grill/broiler.

Push about 3 pork pieces onto each soaked skewer. Cook in the preheated oven for about 18 minutes, or under the preheated grill/broiler for 12–15 minutes, until well browned.

For the dipping sauce, mix all the ingredients in a bowl with 4 tablespoons hot water.

For the noodle salad, put the rice vermicelli, a pinch of salt and a dash of vinegar in a bowl or pan of boiling water, cover and let cook for 5–10 minutes, until soft. Drain and rinse with hot water.

Mix together the herbs, lettuce and cucumber and divide between 4 bowls. Add the noodles, pickle and pickled leeks, if using, on top. Scatter the peanuts over everything. Serve with the pork skewers and dipping sauce.

PAD THAI IS WIDELY AVAILABLE THESE DAYS, BUT THE UBIQUITOUS SICKLY-SWEET TAKE-AWAY IS NOTHING LIKE THE FRESH, VIBRANT DISH FOUND ALL OVER THAILAND. IN THEORY IT SEEMS A RELATIVELY SIMPLE DISH, IN PRACTICE, HOWEVER, IT IS QUITE EASY FOR IT TO TURN INTO A CONGEALED, UNDER-SEASONED LUMP. THE EASIEST WAY TO AVOID THIS IS TO KEEP SEPARATING THE NOODLES WHILE COOKING TO AVOID THEM STICKING TOGETHER.

PAD THAI

SAUCE
4 tablespoons fish sauce (or light soy sauce if you're vegetarian)
3 tablespoons coconut palm sugar
1½ tablespoons tamarind paste mixed with 1½ tablespoons water or 3 tablespoons freshly squeezed lime juice
200 g/6½ oz. flat rice noodles

vegetable oil
100 g/3½ oz. pak choi/bok choy, leaves separated and sliced lengthways
3 garlic cloves
100 g/1⅓ cups beansprouts
1 fresh red chilli/chile, seeded, ½ chopped and ½ finely sliced
6 spring onions/scallions, finely sliced
2 eggs, beaten

TO SERVE
handful coriander/cilantro leaves
50 g/2 oz. cashews or peanuts, roasted
lime wedges

SERVES 2

To make the sauce, place the fish sauce, coconut palm sugar and tamarind or lime juice in a small saucepan and place over a medium heat. Warm through until the sugar dissolves completely then remove from the heat.

Soak the noodles in hot water for approximately 5–7 minutes until tender, but not soft.

Put 2 tablespoons of vegetable oil in a large frying pan/skillet or wok over a high heat. Add in the pak choi/bok choy, garlic, beansprouts, the chopped chilli/chile and 4 of the spring onions/scallions. Stir-fry for about 1 minute until the garlic is aromatic, keeping an eye on it so it does not burn. Add the noodles to the pan with 1 tablespoon of water, tossing them around and separating any noodles that are sticking together. Add in the sauce and cook, tossing occasionally, until the noodles have soaked up most of the liquid and are cooked through. Taste to make sure.

Push the noodles slightly over to the side to make way for the beaten egg. Scramble it in the pan and stir through the noodles. Taste, and if necessary, add more seasoning. Plate up with the remaining spring onions/scallions, sliced chilli/chile, coriander/cilantro and cashew nuts sprinkled over the top. Serve immediately with the lime wedges on the side.

IT'S RARE TO TURN A CORNER IN THAILAND WITHOUT SEEING A NOODLE SOUP VENDOR, SO MUCH SO, IT SOON BECOMES A DAILY DISH IN THE DIET OF RESIDENTS AND TOURISTS ALIKE. THE TRADITIONAL VEGETABLE NOODLE SOUP USES MUNG BEAN OR THREAD NOODLES (SOMETIMES CALLED GLASS OR CELLOPHANE NOODLES), BUT YOU COULD SUBSTITUTE ANY RICE NOODLES.

MUNG BEAN VEGETABLE NOODLE SOUP

375 g/13 oz. mung bean noodles or rice vermicelli noodles
1 tablespoon toasted sesame oil
1 tablespoon vegetable oil
8 garlic cloves, crushed
1 tablespoon finely chopped galangal, or fresh root ginger
2 litres/quarts vegetable stock or water
2 tablespoons vegan fish sauce, or soy sauce or tamari
3 tablespoons light soy sauce, or tamari
1 teaspoon soft brown sugar
1 stick of lemongrass, bruised with a rolling pin
100 g/3½ oz. shredded white cabbage
100 g/3½ oz. shredded dark green cabbage or kale
1 carrot, coarsely grated or cut into julienne
120 g/2 cups beansprouts
4 spring onions/scallions, sliced
freshly squeezed juice of 1 lime
2 red chillies/chiles, finely sliced, to garnish

Serves 3–4

Put the noodles in a large bowl and cover with boiling water. Leave for 4–5 minutes until the noodles are soft. Rinse, drain and set aside.

Heat the sesame and vegetable oils in a large pan over medium heat and cook the garlic and galangal for 3–4 minutes, until golden brown and starting to crisp. (At this stage, you can put the crispy fried garlic and galangal back into a mortar, bash them a little to make a rough paste, if you like, then return to the pan. Or leave whole, for texture.) Add the vegetable stock and bring to a boil. Add the vegan fish sauce, soy sauce, sugar and bruised lemongrass. Bring to a boil, then simmer for 5 minutes.

Add the shredded cabbages, carrot, beansprouts, three-quarters of the chopped spring onions/scallions and the noodles, then return to the boil and immediately remove from the heat.

Remove the lemongrass and add the lime juice. To serve, pour into large, deep bowls and top each bowl with the remaining spring onions/scallions and sliced chillies/chiles.

DEEP-FRIED FRUIT IS A COMMON SNACK IN SOUTH-EAST ASIA, WITH LOTS OF VARIATIONS OF BATTER. THIS CRISPY COCONUT BATTER IS NATURALLY GLUTEN-FREE, AND THE STICKY CARAMEL IS WORTH TRYING!

BANANA & PINEAPPLE FRITTERS

For the caramel, put 60 ml/¼ cup water in a heavy-bottomed pan with the glucose and sugar. Stir to help dissolve the sugar, then gently bring to a simmer over medium heat, without stirring. You want to avoid the formation of sugar crystals. It is also important not to stir the mixture once it is heating. Swirl the pan to encourage the sugar to dissolve. Heat until the mixture is clear, then turn up the heat slightly and simmer until it becomes deep brown (but not burnt). This can take 10–15 minutes. Remove from the heat, then carefully beat in the coconut milk. It will bubble, so take care. Add the orange blossom water and stir well. The caramel can be stored in a glass bottle in the fridge for 1 month.

To make the batter, put the flours in a large bowl and add the sugar, salt and coconut. Stir in 300 ml/ generous 1¼ cups water to make a thick batter.

Gently reheat the caramel sauce in a small pan over a medium–low heat until warm, if prepared in advance. Preheat the oven to 110°C (225°F) Gas ¼ and put a baking sheet in to warm. Heat the oil for deep-frying in a wok or a large, heavy-bottomed pan over medium heat. Test the oil with a little batter mix, to ensure that it sizzles.

Cooking in batches, dip the prepared fruit in the batter, then gently lay them in the hot oil. Fry until golden brown. Drain on kitchen paper/paper towels and keep warm on a baking sheet while you cook the remaining batches. Serve the hot-and-crispy fruit pieces drizzled with the caramel sauce.

1 small pineapple, peeled, cored and sliced into rings
6 bananas, peeled and cut in half lengthways

CARAMEL
1 tablespoon liquid glucose, or a pinch of cream of tartar
200 g/1 cup unrefined sugar
300 ml/generous 1¼ cups coconut milk, at room temperature
2–3 teaspoons orange blossom water

BATTER
125 g/1 cup rice flour
4 tablespoons tapioca flour/starch
2 tablespoons caster/ superfine sugar
½ teaspoon salt
50 g/⅔ cup desiccated/dry unsweetened shredded coconut
500 ml/2 cups vegetable oil, for deep-frying

SERVES 4–6

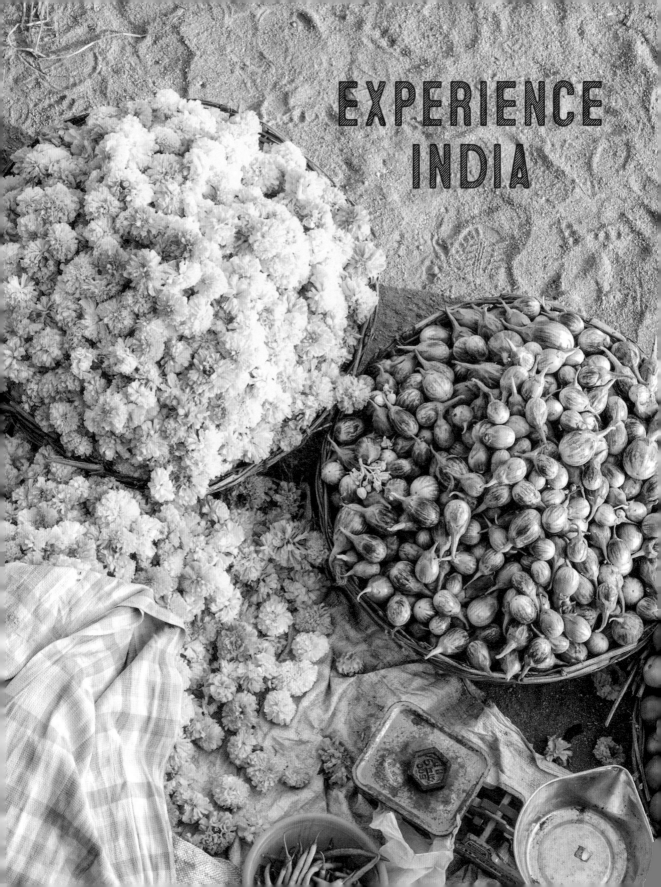

EXPERIENCE
INDIA

STREET FOOD IS A HUGE PART OF THE INDIAN FOOD SCENE AND WHAT'S MOST MAGICAL ABOUT IT IS HOW SO MANY OF THE DISHES ARE VEGETARIAN. THIS RECIPE SHOWCASES THE BEAUTY AND VERSATILITY OF THE HUMBLE POTATO. SPICED MASHED POTATO COATED IN A GRAM/CHICKPEA FLOUR BATTER AND THEN DEEP-FRIED... WHAT'S NOT TO LOVE ABOUT THIS COMFORT FOOD?

BATATA VADAS

vegetable oil, for
   deep-frying
plain/all-purpose flour,
   for dusting
cucumber and mint
   raita, to serve

POTATO FILLING
1 kg/scant 5 cups
   mashed potatoes
   (Maris Piper or Yukon
   Gold)
2 teaspoons Holy Trinity
   Paste (see page 142)
2 teaspoons salt
½ teaspoon ground
   turmeric
1 teaspoon Kashmiri red
   chilli/chili powder
2 teaspoons caster/
   granulated sugar
freshly squeezed juice
   of 1 lemon

SEASONED OIL
3 tablespoons vegetable
   oil
1 teaspoon mustard
   seeds
1 teaspoon sesame seeds
½ teaspoon asafoetida
   power

BATTER
200 g/2¼ cups gram/
   chickpea flour, sifted
½ tablespoon cornflour/
   cornstarch
1 teaspoon ground
   turmeric
1 teaspoon salt

*a baking sheet, lined
   with parchment paper*
*a deep-fat fryer
   (optional)*

SERVES 4–6

Combine all of the ingredients for the potato filling together and mix well.

For the seasoned oil, heat the oil in a small saucepan over medium heat, add the mustard seeds and let sizzle and crackle. Add the sesame seeds, shake around in the pan, then add the asafoetida and stir with a spatula or wooden spoon for 10 seconds. Remove the saucepan from the heat.

Pour the hot seasoned oil into the filling mixture and mix well again.

Shape the mixture into golf-ball-sized pieces, place on the lined baking sheet and put in the fridge to chill.

Mix all of the ingredients for the batter together with 230 ml/scant 1 cup of water and set aside.

Heat the oil for deep-frying in a deep-fat fryer or large, heavy-bottomed pan to 180°C (350°F). Gently roll the balls around in the flour for dusting (in batches of 4–5) and then dip into the batter.

Place the battered balls into the hot oil and deep-fry until they become golden-brown; this should take 4–5 minutes. Drain on kitchen paper/paper towels. Repeat with the rest of the balls.

Serve the batata vadas with tomato, cucumber and mint raita and enjoy!

IT DOES NOT GET MORE 'INDIAN STREET FOOD' THAN SAMOSAS: A SOFT POTATO FILLING WRAPPED IN DOUGH, THEN FRIED TO A SATISFYING CRUNCH. THESE SAMOSAS ARE WONDERFUL SERVED WARM, FRESH OUT OF THE FRYER AND EQUALLY GOOD EATEN COLD FOR LUNCH. YOU CAN TRY USING ANY ROOT VEGETABLE FOR THE FILLING, AS LONG AS IT'S COOKED UNTIL TENDER BEFORE USING TO FILL.

POTATO SAMOSAS

SAMOSA FILLING
4 tablespoons vegetable oil
1 teaspoon cumin seeds
1 1/2 teaspoons coriander seeds, crushed
1/2 teaspoon finely chopped green chilli/ chile
1 teaspoon grated fresh root ginger
350 g/12 oz. boiled, crushed potatoes (Maris Piper or Yukon Gold, boiled and broken; not mashed)
1 teaspoon salt
1/2 teaspoon red chilli/ chili powder
75 g/scant 1/2 cup frozen peas, thawed
1 tablespoon freshly chopped coriander/cilantro

PASTRY
200 g/1 2/3 cups plain/all-purpose flour
1/2 teaspoon ajwain seeds
1/2 teaspoon salt
2 tablespoons melted ghee
60 ml/1/4 cup hot water (not boiling)
vegetable oil, for deep-frying

a deep-fat fryer (optional)

Makes 16 Samosas

For the filling, heat the oil in a pan over medium heat. Add the cumin and fry until sizzling. Add the coriander and fry for 15 seconds. Add the chilli/chile and ginger and fry for 20 seconds. Add the potatoes, salt and chilli/chili powder. Cook until the potatoes are warm, then stir in the peas and coriander/cilantro. Spread the filling on a baking sheet. Let cool.

To make the pastry, put the flour, ajwain seeds and salt in a bowl and mix. Pour in the melted ghee and gently rub in using your fingertips. Next, pour in the hot water, a little at a time, and bring the mixture together to form a dough. Knead until it is smooth with no visible cracks. Cover with some greased clingfilm/plastic wrap and set aside.

To make the pastry sheets for each samosa, divide the dough evenly into eight and roll out to 12.5-cm/5-inch circles. Cut each circle in half.

Build a samosa by making a cone shape with a semi-circle of pastry; bring one side of pastry to overlap with the other and seal the edge together with a bit of water. Gently hold the open cone in one hand and pinch the tip to seal. Using a teaspoon, spoon a little filling into the cone, then use the spoon to gently push in the filling. Leave a lip of pastry (around 1 cm/3/8 inch) to seal; using your fingertips, brush a little water around the inner exposed part of the pastry and seal by pressing the two sides together. Repeat the process to create 16 samosas.

Heat the oil for deep-frying in a deep-fat fryer or large, heavy-bottomed pan to 180°C (350°F). Deep-fry the samosas in batches until golden; about 5–6 minutes. Drain on kitchen paper/paper towels before serving.

AMRITSARI FISH PAKORAS ARE PIECES OF DICED COD COATED IN AN AROMATIC
SPICED BATTER, AND MAKE THE PERFECT APPETIZER FOR ANY INDIAN MEAL OR
SNACK TO ACCOMPANY A BEER! THE CRISPY BATTER COMPLEMENTS THE MOIST,
SUCCULENT FISH TO CREATE A DELICIOUS PAKORA. THESE TASTY TREATS ARE
SO POPULAR THAT THEY ARE NOW EATEN ALL OVER THE INDIA.

AMRITSARI FISH PAKORAS

HOLY TRINITY PASTE
200 g/7 oz. green
  chillies/chiles
200 g/7 oz. garlic
  cloves
200 g/7 oz. fresh root
  ginger
50 ml/3½ tablespoons
  vegetable oil
1 tablespoon salt

500 g/1 lb. 2 oz. cod
  loin, diced into
  2.5-cm/1-inch cubes
plain/all-purpose flour,
  sifted, for dusting
vegetable oil, for
  deep-frying

MARINADE
2 tablespoons
  vegetable oil
1 tablespoon Holy
  Trinity Paste (see
  above)
freshly squeezed juice
  of ½ lemon
½ teaspoon ground
  turmeric
½ teaspoon salt
½ teaspoon chilli/chili
  powder

BATTER
4 tablespoons rice
  flour
8 tablespoons gram/
  chickpea flour, sifted
1 teaspoon ajwain
  seeds
1 teaspoon dried chilli/
  hot red pepper
  flakes
1 teaspoon ground
  turmeric
½ teaspoon baking
  powder
1 tablespoon freshly
  chopped coriander/
  cilantro
180 ml/¾ cup ice-cold
  water
1 teaspoon salt

TO SERVE
mango powder,
  for sprinkling
black salt, for
  sprinkling
sliced chilli/chile
freshly chopped
  coriander/cilantro
lemon wedges

*a deep-fat fryer
  (optional)*

SERVES 4–6

First make the Holy Trinity Paste. Blitz together
the ingredients in a food processor to form a coarse
paste. Set aside and refrigerate. It will keep for up
to 2 weeks.

Rinse the diced fish under cold running water
and gently pat dry.

Combine all of the ingredients for the marinade
together and mix with the diced fish. Let the fish
pieces marinate for a minimum of 30 minutes
at room temperature and a maximum of 24 hours
in the fridge.

Combine all of the ingredients for the batter
together, then set aside for 30 minutes to allow the
ingredients and flavours to all come together. It
should be the consistency of double/heavy cream.

Pat the marinated fish pieces in sifted flour and
shake off any excess. Dip the floured fish pieces into
the batter, ensuring that the fish is fully coated in the
batter, with the spices distributed evenly.

Heat the oil for deep-frying in a deep-fat fryer or
large, heavy-bottomed pan to 180°C (350°F). Deep-fry
the fish pieces in batches of 6–8 pieces until golden-
brown and the fish is cooked through; this should
take no longer than 3–4 minutes per batch. Sprinkle
over a pinch of mango powder and black salt, to
taste, then serve with sliced chilli/chile, chopped
coriander/cilantro and lemon wedges.

MOST COUNTRIES HAVE THEIR VERSION OF A WRAP; THE MEXICANS HAVE BURRITOS, THE JAPANESE HAVE SUSHI ROLLS AND THE INDIANS HAVE THE KATHI ROLL: A ROTI BREAD DIPPED IN BEATEN EGG, SPREAD WITH ANY FILLING AND THEN ROLLED. AN EGG-FRIED WRAP!

PULLED TANDOORI LAMB KATHI ROLL

To make the filling, heat the oil in a heavy-bottomed saucepan over medium heat and fry the cumin seeds until sizzling. Add the ginger and fry until it browns lightly. Add the onion and salt and fry gently until the onion softens. Next, fry the Holy Trinity Paste until it has completely lost its raw aroma. Add all of the ground spices and fry gently to cook them out. If the pan is drying out slightly, you can add a splash of water.

Next, add the tomatoes, mix well, reduce the heat slightly and cover with a lid. Simmer for 15 minutes, stirring every 5 minutes and allowing the tomatoes to gently melt down and form a sauce. Add the tomato purée/paste, stir and add 200 ml/3/4 cup of water and mix well. Add the pulled cooked lamb meat (or whatever meat you would like to use), mix well and simmer for an additional 10 minutes. The sauce should have thickened with the lamb meat to form a filling. Set aside until required.

The kathi rolls are best eaten when prepared at the very last minute, so only fry as many wraps as required.

To make the egg-fried wraps, beat together the eggs and turmeric, then pour onto a large, shallow plate. Dip a roti into the mixture so that it is well-coated on both sides. Shallow-fry on both sides until the egg is cooked. Repeat for the remaining breads.

Assemble the kathi wraps by first spooning on the lamb mixture and then drizzling over a little raita. Wrap each kathi roll tightly and leave one end open so that you can see the filling inside. Serve immediately with the remaining raita alongside.

4 tablespoons vegetable oil, plus extra for shallow-frying
1 teaspoon cumin seeds
1 tablespoon diced fresh root ginger
1/2 red onion, sliced
1/2 teaspoon salt
1/2 teaspoon Holy Trinity Paste (see page 142)
1/2 teaspoon ground cumin
1/2 teaspoon ground coriander
1/2 teaspoon ground turmeric
2 tomatoes, chopped (core and seeds removed)

1 tablespoon tomato purée/paste
250 g/9 oz. pulled cooked lamb meat (or any other leftover meat)
cucumber and mint raita, to serve

EGG-FRIED WRAPS
4 eggs
1/2 teaspoon ground turmeric
4 roti breads (tortilla wraps work just as well)

SERVES 4

CHANNA DHAL FRITTERS, OR DHAL VADAS, MAKE A GREAT NIBBLE OR APPETIZER.
SPICED LENTILS FORMED INTO DEEP-FRIED PATTIES SHOWCASE HOW VERSATILE LENTILS
ARE. THEIR BEAUTY IS THAT THE OUTER LAYER IS CRISPY; THE INNER REMAINING SOFT.

CHANNA DHAL FRITTERS

HARIYALI CHUTNEY

100 g/3½ oz. freshly chopped
    coriander/cilantro
35 g/1 oz. freshly chopped mint
    leaves
2 green chillies/chiles
freshly squeezed juice of
    1½ limes
1 teaspoon fine sea salt
2 heaped teaspoon desiccated/
    dried shredded coconut
1.5-cm/½-inch piece of fresh
    ginger, peeled
1 tablespoon natural/plain yogurt
1 teaspoon caster/granulated
    sugar
4 tablespoons vegetable oil
1 teaspoon cumin seeds, toasted

FRITTERS

200 g/7 oz. channa dhal, picked
    and rinsed, then soaked in
    750 ml/3¼ cups boiling water
    (leave in water for 4 hours)
vegetable oil, for deep-frying,
    plus extra for greasing
½ teaspoon fine sea salt
1 teaspoon peeled and grated
    fresh ginger
1 teaspoon chopped green
    chillies/chiles
¼ teaspoon asafoetida powder
½ teaspoon ground turmeric
5–6 fresh coriander/cilantro
    stems, roughly chopped
¼ onion, finely chopped
Hariyali Chutney (see above),
    to serve

MAKES 10

First, make the Hariyali Chutney. Blitz together all the ingredients, apart from the cumin seeds, in a food processor. Stir in the cumin seeds and set aside or cover and refrigerate. It will keep for up to 3 days.

Drain the soaked dhal and discard the soaking water. Remove 2 heaped tablespoons of the soaked dhal and set aside in a bowl until required.

Using a food processor, blitz together the remaining channa dhal until all of the lentils are coarsely blended and form a paste. Add up to 5 tablespoons of cold water (one at a time) while the mixture is blending, if needed, to help process the mixture. Set aside.

Heat the vegetable oil for deep-frying in a deep-fat fryer or large, heavy-bottomed saucepan to 180°C (350°F).

Meanwhile, transfer the blended lentil paste to a mixing bowl and add all the rest of the ingredients, including the reserved whole dhal. Mix well to form a thick fritter batter.

Grease your hands with a little cold oil and then shape the mixture into 10 equal fritters, roughly about 5–6-cm/2–2½-inches in diameter, 1.5-cm/⅝-inch in height and weighing about 55 g/2 oz. each. A good tip is to shape them into balls to start with, then flatten each one a little between your palms so that they look like patties; slightly thicker in the middle and thinner at the edges.

Check that the oil is hot by dropping in a teaspoon of the mixture; if it stays in one lump and rises to the surface, then the oil is ready. One by one, carefully lower half of the fritters into the oil, ensuring they do not touch. Don't be tempted to touch the fritters until they have turned golden and sealed all over, otherwise they may break. Deep-fry the fritters for about 10–12 minutes, turning a few times until they are evenly golden brown and crunchy.

Drain the fritters on kitchen paper/paper towels and deep-fry the remaining batch. Serve the fritters warm with the Hariyali Chutney or coconut chutney.

ONION BHAJIS ALWAYS SEEMS TO MAKE THEIR WAY ONTO THE LIST OF MUST-HAVES FOR A CURRY TAKE-OUT DINNER. SIMILAR TO A FRITTER, VARIATIONS ARE EATEN ACROSS THE INDIAN SUBCONTINENT AS A STREET FOOD OR AN ENTRÉE TO MAIN DISHES. THIS STELLAR VERSION OF THE DISH IS THE PERFECT WAY TO MAKE USE OF A FEW EXTRA COURGETTES/ ZUCCHINI THAT YOU MIGHT HAVE LEFT OVER IN YOUR FRIDGE.

COURGETTE & ONION BHAJIS

250 g/1 cup soy or Greek yogurt
1 tablespoon pure maple syrup
1 teaspoon sumac
sea salt
450 g/1 lb. courgette/zucchini, coarsely grated
70 g/1/2 cup gram/chickpea flour
40 g/1/3 cup rice flour
2.5-cm/1-inch piece of fresh ginger, peeled and finely grated
2 garlic cloves, peeled and crushed
1 teaspoon ground coriander
1/2 teaspoon cumin seeds
1/2 teaspoon fennel seeds
1/2 teaspoon mustard seeds
175 g/6 oz. red onion, peeled, halved and thinly sliced
1 teaspoon sea salt
small handful fresh coriander/ cilantro, chopped, plus extra to serve
vegetable oil
1 tablespoon pomegranate molasses

SERVES 4

In a bowl combine together the yogurt, pure maple syrup, sumac and a pinch of salt and set aside.

Place the grated courgette/zucchini in a sieve/strainer and press firmly to remove as much liquid as possible, then wrap in a clean tea/kitchen towel and press firmly again to dry them off.

Place the gram/chickpea and rice flours into a large bowl and beat in 80–100 ml/5–6 tablespoons of water to create a thick batter the consistency of double/heavy cream. Add in the ginger, garlic, spices, onion, set-aside courgette/zucchini, 1 teaspoon sea salt, most of the fresh coriander/cilantro and combine well.

Pour 2.5 cm/1 inch of vegetable oil into a frying pan/ skillet and set over a medium–high heat and heat to 180°C (350°F). You test the heat by dropping in a tiny amount of batter – if it turns golden and crisp after about 40 seconds it's ready.

Carefully place separate heaped tablespoons of the mixture into the hot oil, shaping into circular mounds. Do not overcrowd the pan/skillet as it will bring the temperature of the oil down. Fry, turning once or twice until crisp and golden. Remove and drain on kitchen paper/paper towels. Keep the bhajis warm while you fry the rest of them.

Serve immediately with the extra coriander/cilantro sprinkled on top. Dollop the sumac yogurt and pomegranate molasses generously over each crispy bhaji.

OOTHAPAM IS A THICKISH PANCAKE ROBUST ENOUGH TO HOLD A VEGETABLE FILLING AND EASY TO EAT ON THE GO. PEOPLE OFTEN SAY IT LOOKS LIKE A PIZZA, BUT IT DEFINITELY DOESN'T TASTE LIKE ONE! HERE, THERE ARE TWO BATTERS TO CHOOSE FROM, DEPENDING ON THE TIME YOU HAVE.

OOTHAPAM VEGETABLE PANCAKE

TRADITIONAL BATTER
300 g/heaping 1½ cups basmati rice, rinsed until the water runs clear, then drained
100 g/generous ½ cup hulled whole urad dal
½ teaspoon fenugreek seeds
½ teaspoon salt

QUICK BATTER
300 g/2 cups coarse semolina flour
300 g/1⅓ cups soy yogurt
1 teaspoon freshly squeezed lemon juice
1 teaspoon bicarbonate of soda/ baking soda
1 teaspoon salt
pinch of asafoetida powder

vegetable oil, for frying
1–2 green chillies/chiles, to taste, thinly sliced
3 fresh or dried curry leaves, chopped
1 red onion, thinly sliced
2 tomatoes, finely chopped
1 carrot, grated
a small handful of chopped kale
coconut chutney or spicy sambar chilli/chile paste, to serve

MAKES 10–14

For the traditional fermented batter, put the rice in one bowl and the dal and fenugreek seeds in another bowl, and add water to cover by at least 5 cm/2 inches. Soak for at least 6 hours or overnight.

Drain the rice and dal mixtures, reserving both the drained liquids. Put the rice in a food processor or blender and blitz until smooth, adding about 6–7 tablespoons of the soaking water, or more if needed. Repeat with the dal mixture, adding 5 tablespoons of the soaking water and blending until smooth.

Put both mixtures in a large bowl. Mix together with the salt and cover with clingfilm/plastic wrap. Leave overnight in a warm place to ferment. The batter will keep for up to 1 week in the fridge once it is fermented, or can be frozen for up to six months.

For the quick batter, mix all the ingredients together with enough water to make a thick pouring consistency. Set aside for 10–15 minutes.

If using the fermented batter, add a little more water as necessary to make a thick pouring consistency.

Add ½ tablespoon oil to a large non-stick frying pan/skillet over medium heat. Using a ladle, spoon the batter into the centre of the pan and use the back of the ladle to smooth it out to the edges. Add a little oil around the edge to ensure it doesn't stick.

Quickly remove the pan from the heat and scatter the top of the pancake with some of the prepared vegetable topping ingredients. Use the back of the ladle to push the vegetables slightly into the batter. Return the pan to the heat and cook for 3 minutes, until the pancake begins to brown underneath, then turn it over and cook for another 1–2 minutes. Repeat to make the remaining pancakes. Serve immediately with the suggested accompaniments.

KAALI DHAL LITERALLY TRANSLATES TO BLACK
DHAL. SAVOURY, MOREISH AND ACCENTED WITH
A RICH SAUCE, IT IS A HOMELY INDIAN DISH FOR
WHEN YOU NEED SOMETHING TO KEEP YOU GOING.

KAALI DHAL

SEASONED OIL
5 tablespoons vegetable oil
5 cardamom pods
5 cloves
a 5-cm/2-inch cinnamon stick
1 teaspoon cumin seeds
1 teaspoon red chilli/chili powder
2 green chillies/chiles, slit

300 g/1½ cups urad dhal, soaked
 in 2 litres/quarts water overnight
100 g/generous ½ cup dried red
 kidney beans, soaked in 2 litres/
 quarts water overnight
5 tablespoons vegetable oil
1 tablespoon ginger paste
1 tablespoon garlic paste
1 onion, finely chopped
1 teaspoon salt
1 teaspoon Holy Trinity Paste (see
 page 142)
½ teaspoon each of ground
 coriander, ground cumin and
 ground turmeric
1 teaspoon tomato purée/paste
3 large tomatoes, chopped (core
 and seeds removed)
50 g/3½ tablespoons butter
2 tablespoons double/heavy cream
1 teaspoon dried methi/fenugreek
 leaves
1 tablespoon freshly chopped
 coriander/cilantro
1 teaspoon garam masala
Seasoned Oil (see above)
roti breads, to serve

a pressure cooker

SERVES 6

First, prepare the Seasoned Oil. Heat the oil in a small pan, add
the cardamom pods, cloves and cinnamon. Fry for a minute, then
add the cumin seeds and fry until sizzling. Add the remaining
ingredients and fry for an additional 10–15 seconds. Let cool.

Drain and rinse the soaked lentils and kidney beans, then
transfer to a pressure cooker with 1.5 litres/quarts of the water. Cook
until the lentils are falling apart; about 3–4 whistles (or 15 minutes)
depending on your pressure cooker guidelines. (Alternatively, you
can boil them in a pan, but this can take up to 4 hours.)

Heat the oil in a pan over low–medium heat and fry the ginger
and garlic pastes until the shreds begin to separate from one
another. Add the onion and salt and fry well so that the onions
are soft and golden-brown; this will take a good 30 minutes.

Now that we have created a caramelized base flavour to the
sauce, add the Holy Trinity Paste to add a fresh heat in the dish. Fry
the paste in the onion mix for 3–4 minutes. Add the ground spices
and cook for 3–4 minutes; add a splash of water if the pan starts to
dry out. Add the tomato purée/paste, mix well and fry for 2 minutes,
then add the tomatoes and mix again. Cover with a lid and gently
simmer to allow the tomatoes to melt down to form a rich sauce.

Add the cooked lentils and mix really well. Loosen the sauce
with more of water to your desired consistency.

To increase the richness, add the butter, double/heavy cream,
dried fenugreek leaves, freshly chopped coriander/cilantro and
garam masala. Mix well and let the dhal slowly simmer on an
extremely low heat for 10–15 minutes.

Pour the Seasoned Oil on top of the dhal, scraping every last bit
out. Mix well, and serve immediately with fresh roti breads.

KOFTAS HAVE MANY NAMES DEPENDING ON WHAT THEY ARE MADE FROM.
WHEN IT COMES TO A STREET FOOD TRAILER, THE NAME WILL ALSO DEPEND
ON WHERE THEY ARE BEING SERVED - THE FESTIVAL TREND IS FOR PUNS
THESE DAYS, SO YOU'LL BE ASKING FOR A 'DUDE, WHERE'S MY KOFTA?'

KOFTA MASALA

120 g/1 cup cashew
  nuts
2 bottle/doodhi
  gourds, peeled and
  grated
375 g/3 cups gram/
  chickpea flour
2 large red chillies/
  chiles
1 teaspoon ginger
  paste
1 teaspoon garlic paste
a large handful of
  fresh coriander/
  cilantro
1 teaspoon chaat
  masala
1 teaspoon salt
vegetable oil, for
  shallow-frying
steamed basmati rice,
  to serve

MASALA SAUCE
2 aubergines/
  eggplants, roughly
  chopped
1 teaspoon salt
2 tablespoons
  vegetable oil, plus
  extra to grease
2 onions, thinly sliced

1 tablespoon ginger
  paste
1 tablespoon garlic
  paste
½ teaspoon ground
  turmeric
1 teaspoon ground
  cumin
2 teaspoons ground
  coriander
1 teaspoon Kashmiri
  chilli/chili powder,
  or ½ teaspoon chilli/
  chili powder and 1½
  teaspoons paprika
4 small green chillies/
  chiles, finely
  chopped
2 x 400-g/14-oz. cans
  chopped tomatoes
1 teaspoon garam
  masala
1 heaped tablespoon
  dried methi/
  fenugreek leaves, or
  ½ bunch of fresh
  leaves, roughly
  chopped

SERVES 4–6

Toast the cashew nuts in a dry pan/skillet over medium heat for 1–2 minutes, stirring occasionally, until golden. Put the grated gourds in a colander and drain the excess liquid, squeezing to remove as much water as possible. Put the flour in a bowl and add the chillies/chiles, cashews, ginger and garlic pastes, fresh coriander/cilantro, chaat masala and salt. Add 240–360 ml/1–1½ cups of water to form a thick paste. Taste the paste and add more salt if necessary.

Half-fill a frying pan/skillet with oil and place over medium heat. Wet your hands and form the mixture into 16–18 balls each about the size of a golf ball. In batches, gently drop the koftas into the oil and fry until golden brown and cooked through. Drain on kitchen paper/paper towels.

Preheat the oven to 220°C (425°F) Gas 7.

To make the masala sauce, put the aubergines/eggplants on a greased baking sheet and sprinkle over the salt. Roast for 20–30 minutes until browned. Heat the oil in a large pan over medium heat and cook the onions for 5 minutes, until softened. Add the ginger, garlic, spices and fresh chillies/chiles, then fry for 3 minutes more. Add the tomatoes and garam masala. Bring to a boil, then simmer gently for 10–15 minutes until thickened.

Add the aubergines/eggplants and simmer for 10 minutes, until the mixture is thick. Using a stick blender, blend until smooth. Add the methi/fenugreek and stir well. Season with more salt if necessary. Add the koftas and simmer gently, being careful not to break the koftas. Serve with steamed basmati rice.

KULFI IS THE INDIAN EQUIVALENT OF ICE CREAM AND IS A VERY POPULAR AND TRADITIONAL DESSERT CHOICE THAT IS SERVED ALL YEAR ROUND, BUT EATS VERY WELL DURING THE HOT SUMMER MONTHS! IT IS MEANT TO BE DENSER, HEAVIER AND CREAMIER THAN ICE CREAM, WHICH IS WHY CONDENSED MILK IS USED, AS IT ADDS A LOVELY, RICH AND THICK MOUTHFEEL. THIS RECIPE ALSO USES SAFFRON THAT ADDS A WARM FRAGRANCE.

MANGO & MINT KULFI

3–4 saffron strands
500 ml/2 cups full-fat/whole milk
100 ml/⅓ cup condensed milk
50 g/¼ cup caster/granulated sugar
2 teaspoons cornflour/cornstarch, dissolved in a little warm water
100 ml/⅓ cup double/heavy cream
200 ml/¾ cup mango purée
15 large mint leaves, finely chopped, plus extra to serve

TO SERVE
chopped pistachio nuts
dried rose petals

SERVES 6

Soak the saffron strands in 2 tablespoons of the milk.

Meanwhile, pour the rest of the milk into a pan with the condensed milk and sugar, and gently bring to a boil. Simmer for 1 hour, stirring occasionally so that the mixture does not stick to the pan.

Once it has reduced by half, stir in the dissolved cornflour/cornstarch, ensuring that there are no lumps, and beat into the hot kulfi mix. Simmer for 2 minutes, stirring occasionally and making sure that the mix does not stick to the pan. Add the double/heavy cream and saffron strands in milk. Mix in well.

Remove the pan from the heat and let cool until the mix is no longer warm. Test with a clean finger.

Next, add the mango purée and the chopped mint and stir well to distribute the ingredients evenly. Transfer to a pouring jug/pitcher and pour into the desired serving dishes or moulds. Freeze for 2–3 hours.

Serve straight from the freezer, sprinkled with extra mint, chopped pistachio nuts and dried rose petals for decoration.

INDEX

RECIPE CREDITS

Valerie Aikman-Smith
Salt & Pepper Squid

Brontë Aurell
Beef Burgers
Sausage Rolls

Miranda Ballard
Dry Rubbed Pulled Pork
Pizzettes

Ghillie Basan
Deep-fried Mussels
Deep-fried Whitebait
Hot Hummus with Pine
Nuts & Chilli Butter
Spicy Carrot & Chickpea
Tagine

Jordan Bourke
Baklava
Courgette & Onion Bhajis
Pad Thai
Socca Pancakes

Maxine Clark
Corned Beef & Sweet Potato
Pasties

Ursula Ferrigno
Pistachio Ice Cream
Potato Croquettes

**Ben Fordham & Felipe
Fuentes Cruz**
Chicken Quesadillas
Fish Tacos
Fried Tortilla with Black Beans
Slow-cooked Beef Burrito
Tamales

Dunja Gulin
Traditional Chickpea Falafel
Pockets

Carol Hilker
Egg Rolls
Elotes (Grilled Corn)
Jerk Wings
Red Hot Buffalo Wings

Vicky Jones
Korean Moong Pancakes
with Pork

Jackie Kearney
Banana & Pineapple Fritters
with Orange Blossom
Caramel
Kofta Masala
Mung Bean Noodle Soup
Oothapam Vegetable Pancake
Twice-cooked Tempeh

Jenny Linford
Crispy Garlic Chive Chicken
Wontons
Jollof Rice
Potato, Cheese & Chive
Pierogi
Saffron Garlic Chicken Kebabs
Yakitori-glazed Mushroom &
Chicken Skewers

Loretta Liu
Traditional Shrimp Dumplings
Vegetable Clamshell Bao Buns

Uyen Luu
BBQ Pork-belly Skewers
Lemongrass Beef Baguette
Mackerel Ceviche
Sizzling Crêpes with Pork
& Prawns
Spring Rolls

Jane Mason
Bulgarian Cheese Bread

Theo A. Michaels
Filled Crispy Filo Rolls
Vegetable Tempura

Hannah Miles
Churros with Hot Chocolate
Sauce
Popcorn Doughnuts

Miisa Mink
Nordic Open Sandwiches

Nitisha Patel
Amritsari Fish Pakoras
Batata Vadas
Channa Dhal Fritters
Kaali Dhal
Mango & Mint Kulfi
Potato Samosas
Pulled Tandoori Lamb
Kathi Roll

Louise Pickford
Alter-ego Sushi
Chicken & Seafood Paella

Chicken Laksa
Ramen with Tempura Prawns
Salmon & Spring Onion Gyoza

James Porter
Poke Inari Cups

Annie Rigg
Patatas Bravas
Sole Goujons & Chips
Spiced Fried Chicken

Laura Washburn Hutton
Curry Fries
Halloumi & Za'atar Fries

PICTURE CREDITS

Tim Atkins 80
Jan Baldwin 53, 79, 83, 84
Steve Baxter 41, 49.
Peter Cassidy 1, 16, 18, 23, 29,
30, 33, 34, 45, 64–65, 69, 87,
160
Tara Fisher 92, 131, 148
Louise Hagger 102, 105
Mowie Kay 10, 11, 61, 98
Erin Kunkel 116
Adrian Lawrence 101
William Lingwood 37, 73
David Munns 62, 74
Steve Painter 15, 42,
46, 50, 58, 91
William Reavell 109
Christopher Scholey 108
Toby Scott 19, 20, 26
Ian Wallace 54, 106, 120, 123
Kate Whitaker 70
Clare Winfield 2, 3, 12, 66, 88,
89, 97, 112–115, 117, 119, 121, 124,
127, 128, 132, 135, 139, 140,
143–147, 151, 152, 155, 156

Travel photography:
4l holgs/Getty Images
4r REDA&CO/Getty Images
5 117 Imagery/Getty Images
6l JordanBert/istock
6c Bashir Osman's
Photography/Getty Images
6f Getty Images
7l MeogiaPhoto/ Getty
Images
7c Kaveh Kazemi/Getty
Images
7r Image Professionals
GmbH/Alamy Stock Photo
8–9 CHUYN/Getty Images
13 Jeffrey Isaac Greenberg 8/
Alamy Stock Photo
21 National Geographic Image
Collection/Alamy Stock Photo
24–25 reisegraf.ch/Alamy
Stock Photo
27a DarrenTierney/Getty
Images
27c Margie Politzer/Getty
Images
28 Ricardo Ceppi/Getty
Images
32 David Litschel/Alamy Stock
Photo
38–39 INNA FINKOVA/Alamy
Stock Photo
40 espana/Alamy Stock Photo
44 Alena Kravchenko/Alamy
Stock Photo
48 poludziber/Getty Images
52l Mikel Bilbao/VW PICS/
Getty Image
52r dvoevnore/Getty Images
56–57 ivanoel28/Getty
Images
59 Pawel Kazmierczak/Alamy
Stock Photo
63 Jason Wallengren
Photography/Stockimo/
Alamy Stock Photo

65 insert robertharding/
Alamy Stock Photo
71 Tim E White/Alamy Stock
Photo
72 Alex Craig/Getty Images
75 Pascal Preti/Getty Images
76–77 Julio Etchart/ullstein
bild via Getty Images
78l Chalffy/Getty Images
78r Edwin Remsberg/Getty
Images
81 Nick Brundle Photography/
Getty Images
85 Marco Bottigelli/Getty
Images
86 Jacqueline Nguyen/Alamy
Stock Photo
90 Chris Griffiths/Getty
Images
94–95 Cristina Pedrazzini/
Getty Images
103 kiszon pascal/Getty
Images
110–111 Christian Kober/Getty
Images
118 Ed Freeman/Getty Images
129 Judy Bellah/Getty Images
130 Holger Leue/Getty Images
134 Yaowalak
Pattanatheeraboon /EyeEm/
Getty Images
136–137 Tim Gainey / Alamy
Stock Photo
138 Junaid Bhat/Getty Images
141 Mint /Getty Images
150 Sam Spicer/Getty Images
153 LAURENE BECQUART/AFP/
Getty Images